TAPESTRY OF THE SUN

A COLLECTION OF POEMS

CADE NOBLE MADDOX

ACKNOWLEDGEMENTS

Weaving together this book, Tapestry of The Sun, has in some sense been a fated process, for the mythic, heroic, and the poetic have always resonated deeply with me. However, there are many people to whom I owe a great deal of gratitude, for they either supported me or served as inspiration for my work and without whom this book would not be what it is now.

To my father and mother, I owe you thanks that words, no matter the amount of my creative effort, could ever adequately express. Thank you both.

To my friends and extended family, you were often the model for many of my pieces and who not only quietly reside within the pages of this book but, just as importantly, exemplify virtues and live lives worth writing about.

I am likewise thankful to my friend Samuel Morgan for his efforts and continued support in the creation of this work. All of the illustrations, including the cover art, were crafted in collaboration, and it is through Samuel's own talents that this collection is available in its present form. As a note, all illustrations were hand- drawn before being digitally uploaded, ensuring that any resemblance to existing media is incidental.

Throughout the course of this book, I have liberally drawn inspiration from countless sources, and their voices echo within my writing. For example, in A Letter To Women, I allude to Mae West's quote of the curve being more powerful than the sword, and my poem Pitiless Beasts directly draws its inspiration from D. H. Lawrence's poem Self-Pity. There are countless quotes and references embedded in my poetry and I intend no plagiarism nor deception. Every title, line, or reference borrowed from another is intended as a nod—at least, to the original source—or, at most, a sincere tribute of homage. With that said, all of my work is original and any outside influence is synthesized with my own creativity.

There are two contemporaries that I would like to especially acknowledge, as much of my work is directly a byproduct of their work. Jack Donovan and C.B. Robertson have provided me with a wealth of inspiration through their writing, podcasts, and other works, and whose influence undoubtedly shines throughout the pages of this book. It should be noted, however, that the views and opinions expressed in this book do not necessarily reflect those of either aforementioned author. I thank them both for their impact.

Furthermore, as a matter of some significance, I have decided to keep my poems, more or less, in chronological order as they were written, or at least, as the ideas came to me, with some exceptions existing where aesthetic considerations overruled chronology. This ordering I deemed somewhat expressive in its own right, for the natural sequence in which they were written tells, in some sense, another story within the greater tapestry.

Lastly, I am grateful for all the heroes and warriors, writers and poets, men and women, of both past and present within whom I find a bottomless wellspring of imagination and creativity; and to you the reader, I am also indebted, for you give breath to those heroes and poets through emulation, living those heroic tales in your own lives, and ensuring the mythic lives on in flesh and blood.

Forever grateful,
Cade Noble Maddox

CONTENTS

THE AGELESS FIRE OF YOUTH

Never again will I be this young,
With blazing heart and bursting lung,
Aching to unleash my vital force,
Like a prime and spirited wild horse,

Fleeting will I say it's not,
Yet strike I will while the iron hots,
Relishing in the here and now,
For the curse of age I disavow,

While time may come to claim my hand,
My soul forever on this mortal strand,
Shall remain an ageless flame of life,
Where youth is rich and vigor rife,

But now my body matches soul,
Where flesh and spirit form a whole,
Basking in the joys of youth,
Where vitality wears the crown of truth,

For ample is my mighty limb,
My muscles roaring with hearty vim,
And knifelike is my vibrant mind,
A kinetic force when combined,

Towards high ambitions I do hold,

For my pace is proud and my will is bold,
With a purpose moved by fulgent flame,
I pursue the path of my impassioned aim,

Thus intimate is potential's song,
For she loves the youth so bright and strong,
Inspiring in her luscious sway,
While horizons glow and young's the day,

Falling often I but roll,
For all my failures hold little toll,
While anti-fragile is my state,
And every defeat is a gift of fate,

Love and violence I do know,
Each with their wisdom to bestow,
Leaving havoc in their wake,
By which naivetè does blanch and break,

As freedom seems a simple boon,
For across the land I am strewn,
Itinerant as an errant knight,
In longing for the righteous fight,

With a pack of boys I do run,
Howling at the moon and chasing the sun,
Looking for trouble and breaking hearts,
Lost in life's tides of adventure and art,

And as I say the time may pass,
These moments like lightning in a glass,

Ephemeral in their flash and mirth,
Yet never losing their lucent worth,

And always there is life to live,
For the bounty of Being forever gives,
As qualms of age can hold no ground,
Wherever the spirit of youth is found.

INVIOLABLE BROTHERHOOD

A love far greater than a man for his wife,
The love between men deep and profound,
It comes from respect, from hardship and strife,
A love not erotic but with honor abound.

Not through words nor touch does this devotion arise,
Not through perversion nor lust that it flows,
It's the bond of brotherhood such unions symbolize,
From a shared life of both joys and woes.

For the love of a brother is an unbreakable link,
Forged with a holy bond,
It holds you firmly against the brink,
And against the perils of the unknown and beyond.

PLIGHT OF THE PILGRIM

Across desolate deserts and over roaring seas,
Haggard from journey you drop to your knees,
Grim vales before you, alpine farther on,
To the mount, to the summit, for nameless reasons you're drawn.

With weary foot and humble dress,
You trek the ascent, your mighty fall you profess,
To the hope of answers, to the call of salvation,
Perhaps at the peak you'll join with creation.

RELIGIOSITY ETERNAL

From the gods of old, to the father and son,
And from the ancient spirits, thy will be done.
For men of old and the man of now,
Hearken the call, keep sacred the vow.

The wheel of time rolls on and on,
The tree of life still tall and strong,
The cross still sits upon the hill,
The wicked raging against his will.

Hold fast the old and the pure,
Darkness looms, an enticing lure,
But hallowed is the righteous word,
Still in this world of the absurd.

STEADFAST

When you don't know the course ahead,
And the winds do shift and change,
The sails no more than thread,
Keep steadfast at the helm.

When the storm looms before you,
And the wood splinters and cracks,
Though there be no hope of rescue,
Keep steadfast at the helm.

When the wind batters your face,
And the rain floods the deck,
With not a sign of saving grace,
Keep steadfast at the helm.

When all but your grit is lost,
And the ship is staggering on,
Though waves and wind do lash and toss,
You're still steady at the helm.

When the men about you cry with fear,
And look upon your stalwart frame,
They'll see the end is not so clear,
You're still steady at the helm.

When the darkness fades away,

And the land is set in sight,
How bright now is the day,
You're still steady at the helm.

UNITY

Our blood is spilled upon this land,
No matter the creed or race,
We were once one stout and solid band,
United by the pride of Heaven's grace.

THE RITE OF SUPPER

Food gleaned by thy own hands,
Table prepared and waiting,
Men still gather like the ancient bands,
A bond held tight yet liberating.

MAN PRIMEVAL

The cry of the eagle, the bang of the drum,
The roar of the fire and the laughter of men,
With glow of the moon and blaze of the sun,
You dance and you fight in the festive din.

From the brunt of spear and flash of steel,
To zealous chants and pagan rites,
This is Man raw and real,
In these long forgotten primordial nights.

BEST OF TIMES, WORST OF TIMES

The best of times, the worst of times, Is what I always say,
About my days in the Corps and all it brought my way,
With a lot of struggle and a lot of work but with some laugh and play,
I'd go back in a heartbeat, back to my glory days.

WHAT IF?

Long down the path you tread,
Nothing but dirt and stone,
Endless breaks and forks ahead,
Thickets and copse overgrown.

How many trails branch off from sight,
How many roads race far away,
Each one full of distant plight,
Each one leading to a different day.

There are no signs stuck in the mud,
No arrows on the trees,
Just a fire in your blood,
And a wonder of what could be.

Each intersection that you face,
Each crossroad you stumble 'pon,
Steers you towards some unknown place,
Where every alternative is gone.

Trudging onward you must go,
Uncertainty in your midst,
It doesn't matter what you know,
There's always something that you've missed.

For "what if's" fill the track,

And the trails are but a maze,
But there is no going back,
A new path you must blaze.

There is no right nor wrong,
No proper course to take,
Fate is forged by the strong,
For fortune is what they make.

NAKED SKIN

To feel the sun upon naked skin,
Tis not a venture of mortal sin,
But to be as man was before,
Proud and free on earthen floor.

To stride across the verdant land,
No shoes on feet just spear in hand,
Chasing the warmth of a golden sun,
Till day lay claimed and fully won.

THE WARRIOR'S CALL

Boldly charging I race by,
Like lighting cross a blackened sky,
Too mad to care if I live or die,
Towards bloody fray with savage cry.

Cutting cross the frenzied field,
Left arm dons a battered shield,
Gleaming sword in right I wield,
No man or beast gains my yield.

Brothers around me scream and fall,
Ancestors watch me from lofty hall,
Sword is bloody and blunted dull,
Spurred onward, I by the warriors call.

COUNSEL OF COURAGE

The youths huddle round the grizzled man,
Here they congregate to understand,
What's the secret to get a wife so pure,
Asks a youth whose not so sure,
The old man grunts and ponders such a deed,
He spits and nods, tis courage you need.

Another boy thinks then raises his hand,
How's one go to war to make a stand,
The old man laughs that's an easy one,
Courage will hold you and mock those who run.

A third youth stands and brazenly asks,
Are your answers the same for every task,
The old man smiles and thinks back on his life,
Courage, my boy, spurs you through every strife.

LIFE AS ART

To harness the passion of the senses,

Stoking that fire of the heart,

To hell with the consequences,

Your life is a book, it's a play, it's an art.

PARTING WAYS

Let us not pretend that the honeys just been gold,
Nor that the nights so long and dark have been nothing but bitter cold,
Nor should we imagine that the winds have always blown,
Neither should we say that all seeds that could've been were sown,

For in truth the meat and milk have soured,
And not all saplings were nurtured or flowered,
And still some days have been cloudy and pale,
While we've seen men weep and heard women wail,

There's been beasts and dragons galore,
And many a day with flooded ship and not a glimpse of shore,
Many a people have came and went,
And it seems a weight left us worn and bent,

But again let us be truthful in all that we say,
For the honey was still raw and always the nights led to day,
And so by force of great oar the ship drifted on,
And many seeds were planted whose petals felt the dawn,

And in truth the white milk was still frothy and cold,
And many saplings bore fruit that was both rich and bold,
While many days of rain were still filled with delight,
And many of those peoples struggled long in the fight,

Though dragons dented our armor we slayed those beasts on the prowl,

And though stuck on the sea the salty wind licked our brow,
While a great many have left, many have planted their feet,
And though backs are bent from the load we have still not met defeat,

For all in all the time was short but the days were long,
And we know brotherhood runs deep whether the men are here or gone,
And so the paths diverge as the men wander alone,
Yet that bond is forged and unbroken felt by each down to the bone.

IN THE SPIRIT OF YOUR ANCESTORS

I still remember long winter nights and the glow of the torchlight so long
ago,
When men were hard and women soft building cabins deep in the snow,
When the forest stretched to horizon and further still it ran,
And every boy growing up, knew what it took to be a man,

For I tell you now boy those days are past,
For what glows the brightest does not last,
Yet that blood of man that runs so deep,
Still holds an honor that you must keep,

The sun still rises in the east,
The land still swarms with savage beasts,
And here it is you can stake your claim,
For like the men of old you can do the same.

THE PRICE OF INSIGHT

Ignorance is bliss they say,
And naiveté a tranquil state,
But knowledge is now here to stay,
And for peace of mind it's far too late.

A MAN OF MULTITUDES

So it is that I contradict myself,
For I'm a man of many names,
I have quite a few hats upon my rack,
And no two days am I the same,

I have a long arm,
And a mind like the sea,
Eyes bigger than my stomach,
And a heart that beats free,

I like to do this and I like to do that,
I have big ideas and they also have me,
I'm a hot contradiction and a cold paradox,
And every form is a form I can be.

DEFIANCE OF FATE

It's gone, it's past, it's dust, it's ash,
Yet brighter does the fire burn,
Fists clench white, teeth bite and gnash,
And fate is cursed and spurned.

A LIFE OF PASSION

Pain is the whetstone upon which I'm sharpened,
The hammer and anvil with which I'm forged,
Like a call from the gods and ancestors hearkened,
The burn of the fire and the cold of the fjord.

Feel the torrid, tender kiss of pain,
The salty sea of suffering and strife,
Struggle comes like torrential rain,
A biting wind that cuts like a knife.

Bask in all its power and glory,
Marinate in its wretched allure,
For this is not some solemn, tragic story,
But a life of passion proudly endured.

KEEPING THE FIRE

Do not let the fire die,
The night is long and cold
What is left but to defy,
Like the heroes and men of old.

FOR THE HOST

Sun glistened over golden skin,
Iron muscle and sinew poised,
A silence overtook the boisterous din,
As the youth strode through the mass.

All eyes fixed upon the golden man,
His steel shining like the sun,
Sword held steady in his hand,
While across the field came his foe.

Both armies tensed with anxious nerve,
Each champion circling the other,
As man and god alike observed,
The two men clashed in the center.

Sweat poured first then blood was drawn,
The clang of cold metal rang out,
A pitched battle of skill and valiant brawn,

Fought for the honor of the host.

Swords sang with death in their savage strokes,
Shields were rent and splintered,
Till amidst the fighting sword and soul broke,
Pieces spread across the sward.

Without a pause, the youth attacked,
Running the foreign foe through,
The body dropping to its back,
Victorious he stood in the duel.

A riotous cheer broke the ominous air,
As the legion of this man rejoiced,
For the fiend of the foe could not compare,
To golden youth in its dauntless act.

Thus the horde of the enemy wavered,
Their spirit now weakened and bitter,
By the man the gods had favored,
To win glory on the field.

Through a feat of bravery and bloodshed,
Single combat in its throes,
The fates of field and men were led,
By a champion gallantly aglow.

SEMPER PRORSUM

Where else to go but forward,
What else to do but do,
From an unnamed source your spurred,
Till the dawning of the new.

And where shall your fate guide you,
Does the question truly matter,
So long as you hold true,
Every mirage will shatter.

So tighten up your belt,
And pick up your ragged pack,
Make do with what life has dealt,
You're still pressing the attack.

I AM WHO I AM

To do and not ask why,
To go because I must,
To give it a go and a valiant try,
To wear out instead of to rust.

To prove my worth without acclaim,
Ever upward do I move,
But never in need for flashing fame,
Men of honor are enough to approve.

Forever striving to be a hero,
Yet letting wisdom stay my hand,
For that instinct can be as an arrow,
Swift and deadly in its demand.

Continually do I change,
Wondering if there's a stable core,
That is steadfast in its range,
Or if always there is more.

Trying to find the balance,
Between balance and extreme,
For I strive with wild valiance,
Towards vague, ambitious dreams.

To claim excellence in every feat,

And great quality in every deed,
Knowing there's trials that I'll meet,
Where despite it all I don't succeed.

To be a bright light in the dark,
My own soul a raging flame,
For a single blazing spark,
And the sun are one and the same.

To seek the silver lining,
When rain threatens on the cloud,
And then ride that flashing lightning,
Maybe crashing but still proud.

Moving with force and fire,
Yet supple as the sea,
Embracing both love and ire,
For that's what it means to Be.

To wake with the burning dawn,
Chasing the glory of the sun,
Towards more I'm ever drawn,
Till all ideals are won.

For who I am, I give a damn
And in myself I trust,
For I do because I am,
And I go because I must.

SINK OR SWIM

C'est la vie,

It is what it is,

Now you float adrift at sea,

Did a storm blow through and capsize you,

Or was the kraken set 'pon thee?

Did ol' Davy Jones or sirens moans steer you towards the cliffs,

Truth be told it matters not how you came to be bereft.

What matters now dear lad, whether ye be captain or stowaway,

Your ship were raft or ironclad, or it be night or shining day,

Is rather what you'll do right now, in this moment as it stands,

With salt across your furrowed brow and not a sight of land.

You can let the ocean claim you, down to the briny dim,

Or ye can struggle 'gainst the pitiless blue,

Ye can either sink or ye can swim.

GREEN BOOTS: THE BRIGHT AND BOLD

Where the earth pierces the sky and beauty and death intertwine,
Where the wind cracks like a frozen whip, far past the hardy pine,
Where ice and cold are kings on high and not a spark of life does show,
Climbs a man in bright green boots, smashing through the snow.

A desolate climb, a perilous trek and a single minded aim,
Are the closest companions this man knows on the journey to stake his
claim,
The going is rough but he's come this far, the heights are within his view,
And so all that's left for the man in green boots is to simply push on
through.

Yet a storm now gathers, a tempest looms, and danger now knocks at the
gate,
Victory now fades away, veiled by the twisted hands of fate,
But the resolve of man is hardened and the fire of his heart burns wild,
And so the man in bright green boots pushes on determined and beguiled.

Into the shroud of white, into the den of cold,
Straight into the biting blaze of death's heartless hold,
Turn around the voices cry but not for this hardy man,
He answers to himself alone in this bleak and barren land.

Forlorn by his fellows, he steels his brawny will,
The challenge ringing out to test his luck and skill,
Further up, higher still, to the temple of the gods,

Bright green boots keep marching, stoutly defying the odds.

Until the climb did claim him, swallowed by the mount,
For fortune was not with him and the peak he never found,
He could have turned around and another day returned,
But something deep inside him held a fierce and fervent burn.

Now upon that stony pinnacle, that monument of ice,
Lays the body of a man entombed upon the heights,
Immortalized forever with his banner stark and bold,
Bright green boots defiantly raging against the cold.

DEVOURING MOTHER

Stay, stay, stay inside, outside is cruel and cold,
Seek not the wealth of the world only danger lies that way,
Stay, stay, stay with me and together we'll grow old,
Warm is the hearth that I provide, not the daylight harsh and bold.

Here my son is all you need, not the peril of the land,
Comfort and safety is here between each one of my arms,
Hush hush, don't you worry, yes you are a man,
And if you stay right here with me I'll guide and hold your hand.

So stay with me forever, you wouldn't leave me all alone,
There's nothing for you out there but darkness and despair,
And here right beside me you'll have a perfect little throne,
Stay, stay, stay with mother, do not wander far from home.

BEAUTY OF THE FLESH

Be it soft and silky curves of the lady beauty bestowed,
Or hard and calloused muscle of man marching on the road,
The glowing skin of youth not yet marred or fully tested,
Or the experienced lines of old that a good life has fully wrested.

It is mighty fiber and sinew sculpted from the flesh,
Hewn from primordial matter yet once again made fresh,
A shell of mortal substance rooted to the earth,
Yet fused with that godly spark that imparts a higher worth.

A work of art, a weapon, a temple in its time,
Both honored and abused, an exemplar of the prime,
Deep and rich with wisdom in every atom of its build,
With vibrant life and vigor, it holds abundantly filled.

ODE TO THE IMMORTAL STRIKER

Oh that vanguard of manliness and heroism across the span of time,
The banner man of all noble warriors, the ideal, the pinnacle, man at his prime!
Both golden youth and grizzled grey pay reverence to his burning light,
Homage paid on bloody field or round the guarded fires of the night.

Brave walker of that black unknown and slayer of fierce monsters and men,
The bane of that baleful serpent that would devour his home and kin
For that dread and draconic force lurks deep and deathless in the dark,
With a thousand faces and twisted forms and its purpose diabolically stark,

Thus a stalwart and steadfast champion into the jaws of hell will dare,
For both the glory of the fight and to defend that for which he cares,
Fearlessly charging into forlorn frays or holding vigil on distant posts,
He mans the walls around his home or raids far and exotic coasts,

With a band of brothers he holds the line or single-handed if he must,
For when the call to arms does split the air it's in his valiance that he trusts,
Boldly moving like a man possessed yet matchless in his cunning and skill,
No force can fetter his tumultuous might nor quench his blazing will,

For when the fearsome wolves claw at the door, baying for the blood of man,
They'll find within the rugged threshold, the striker with his ax in hand,
As the night will be but a veil of black save for the fire in the fighters gaze,
Cutting through the throng of vermin, till his whole body is red and ablaze,

On ravaged plains you'll see his wake or his burning mark on blackened fields,
A man of violence unrestrained, as fury and wrath are his to wield,
Like a hound bred for chaotic carnage, poised to rip out the pulsing throat,
Stalking through the savage slaughter of the ruinous realm he smote,

With a brilliance of militant mind, he hones his iron art of war,
Lethal as a lone combatant but even more so commanding a corps,
For his martial primacy is peerless, wrought by his devotion to his trade,
A master of tactics and strategy and a sage of both the gun and the blade,

For a warrior does live for the fight, and always a warrior does fight to win,
Relentless in his courageous campaign to completely conquer or defend,
Confidently roaring with righteous rage or cooly plying his grievous craft,
He gallops headlong into the hellish host or stands proudly at the bow of his craft,

That immortal striker with mighty mettle, both a shield and a shimmering sword,
Ageless and universal, he strives to vanquish the villainous horde,
For vae victis sings his own hardened host from his lofty and lustrous halls,
He stands an exemplar of warriors: a hot gun, a cold blade, an impervious wall.

A MAN'S NAME

I carry my name with honor for it is simply not my own,
It is my fathers and his before and is a sigil of our home,
Thus proudly I shall live by it's gauntlet tested code,
Gaining it renown wherever I may roam.

THE INVIOLATE MARK

I met the devil far out in those blackened bluffs,
And it was there that I shook his hand,
He told me it would never be enough,
For I was marked by ambition's brand,

But I only smiled to his great chagrin,
For ambition to me was the greatest sin.

THE ELEMENTAL

Grounded like the stone of the earth,
Fluid like the flow of the sea,
Bold as the flame of the pyre,
Fast as the wind through the tree.

Monument of iron grit,
Force of persistent might,
Raging passion of life,
Graceful whisper of night.

Steady in your standing,
Supple in your path,
Glowing in your passion,
Commanding in your wrath.

An elemental icon,
Varied in your skill,
Harnessing raw power,
Enacting boundless will.

GROUNDED PULSE

Like a stone, grounded,
Heavy roots of the great oak,
Heartbeat of the mount resounded,
Fire of the forge stoked.

STAY SOLAR

No matter the distance of the road,
Nor the perils and pain that the path does hold,
There be always a light so bright and bold,
The blazing sun raging 'gainst the dark and the cold.

You may feel the pain of bone and skin,
Your mind may torment without an end,
But that glorious glow from without and within,
Overpowers it all as you rise and ascend.

Dark and grim may be the way,
An endless march through the brutal fray,
Yet wielder you are of that golden ray,
For Solar you are and always so is the day.

SUNSET IN THE WEST

Whiskey on the breath,
Tobacco in the lip,
Riding straight for death,
With the six shot on his hip.

The sun is dropping fast ahead,
The braves cry their savage call,
Atop a sturdy thoroughbred,
He reaches swiftly for the draw.

The wind is cracked apart,
Smoke rises in the air,
An arrow sticking from his heart,
And not a man left standing there.

TO REAP, YOU MUST SOW

Before you lies the open field,
A sky above both blue and gold,
A bounty of crop for you to yield,
If you live a life both rich and bold.

You can point at the moochers in the shade,
Spit upon those barren plots of land,
Yet the field is a product of what you've made,
And there's much one can do with one's own hands.

Will you kick at the rocks and curse it all,
Or will you sow the seeds for self and kin,
Will you watch and gawk as the sun slowly falls,
Or hold true to the way of self-yoked men?

TRYING TRUMPS REGRET

Ride the lightning of the day,

Bold be the mark of man,

You may crash like thunder in the fray,

But you'll have tried, you'll have tried doing what you can.

NASTY, BRUTISH, AND RAW

Hard and grim the man doth roam,
Toothy grin dripping with blood flecked foam,
Pain a scar bore upon his back,
A life born of struggle 'pon nature's rack.

Calloused and savage with lurid eyes,
And leather skin burnt from scorching skies,
Across barren hills of darkened earth,
Out from a land of savage birth.

Red stained hands and splintered bone,
Calloused flesh weathered by winter's moans,
Gripped by pain yet moved by flame,
Stolid beast of the mortal plane.

THE GIFT

In the cold and rugged hills,
Amidst the leafless, gnarled trees,
The world is deathly still,
As a man sits bloody on his knees.

The frost is deep and hard,
The wind a howling scream,
The land a blackened scar,
The man's eyes a lurid gleam.

Within the cold he waits,
While in his mind he drifts,
Steadfast in his fate,
Seeking out the gift.

FAREWELL

Long have we walked this splintered road,
As the paths we trod do split and break,
But there is nothing here for us to hold,
For us it seems time hath forsake,
But our footprints deepen in the ash,
Remnants of our youthful gaits,
Monuments of a bonded path,
Parted men with different fates,
Now marching stolid across the land,
Brothers known and brothers gone,
Once a single, brazen band,
Yet loyal always when called upon,
So thus the men do walk away,
With a road behind, a path ahead,
For nothing in this world does stay,
Save what we've left within our stead.

STELLAR SCION

Oh fathers and mothers nameless in the night,
Blazing above with undying light,
Watching and guiding while time falls away,
To your celestial souls forever I pray.

FIRE OF HEAVEN

Flames above blaze bright,
Watchful eyes in blackened night,
Host of Heaven's light.

BULL OF THE SUN

You Bull! Born of boiling blood,
Symbol of the storm crawled out from the mud,
Beast of the earth yet son of the sun,
Fiery hand to the grand golden one.

Strike with a fury and rage with the light,
And take into your yoke those lost in the plight,
A maelstrom of wrath yet a beacon of life,
Joyous and mirthful in the tumultuous strife.

Like a titan of yore you roam the land,
Across fertile fields and the barren sand,
You build and you fight, you love and you burn,
For time may be fleeting but Now it's your turn.

A MAN'S REASONS

He toils and labors in the scorch of the day,

Or shoulders his burdens in hard winter fray,

Never complaining nor asking what for,

His reasons will greet him once home through the door.

THE COMING OF THE MARUTS

Self yoked and bold thunder the brawny bulls of God,
Sun drenched and proud they spear down from the sky,
Each mighty hand wielding a flaming rod,
Lords incarnate of that golden power 'pon high!

Come to do battle with the serpent of Nil,
Virulent venom dripping down it's jaw,
Here to swallow man and break his will,
Defying the light and the Father's law.

The host of heaven falling upon the snake,
Lightning steel plunging through scaly hide,
A tempest raging with an earth shattering quake,
The beast limp and dead in the Bulls thunderous stride.

TRANSMUTATION

Perhaps back to the pit you must go,

To lose yourself and find your soul,

For like a snake that must shed its skin,

The dark night of the soul is the rebirth for men.

CRUSADE OF STRENGTH: INJURY STRIKES

The war on weakness will not cease,
No quarter given, not an ounce of peace,
No matter where you are or the pain of your straits,
The black flag raises high in defiance of fate.

Shall you be far from home or 'pon your native hill,
Broken and bloody with naught left but your will,
The fight rages on, Might must conquer the weak,
The war only ends for those ignoble and meek.

Sound out the drums of war and sharpen up your sword,
Here comes another wave of that overwhelming horde,
The bitter pain and blackened pit rally at the head,
Yet damn them all! This fight you'll wage until you're dead.

DRAGON SLAYER

That fated hand of death, that dragon of the pit,
Breathing down your neck, demanding you submit,
A force of darkness and decay, shrouding out the sun,
Raising the victor's flag, proclaiming "It is done."

Yet bloody as you are and beaten to the bone,
There be no cry for quarter nor even a weary moan,
And as you struggle to your feet, comes the dawning of the light,
The dragon bares its teeth, you have not yet begun to fight.

And though the war is never ending and brutal in its wake,
You know that naught is lost, for you shall never break,
With the courage of the hero donned in the light of day,
Up you stand, drawing sword, you've a serpent here to slay.

EXHAUSTION BECKONS THE SERPENT

Here you come again, you devouring brute,
Lingering in shadow like a worm gnawing at the root,
You attack at days end when heavy and limp is the limb,
A herald of desperation and thoughts potently grim.

You slither up from your darkened hole,
With gaping maw claiming weary soul,
Dragging one back to that blackened pit,
Fangs dripping with malice and venomous spit.

Yet you knew not what manner of men be here,
You thought to capitalize on our mortal fear,
But here stands men of raging blood,
Men who refuse to return to the mud.

THE COST OF A FULL LIFE

Grab the charging bull by its fatal horns,
Ride the lightning from the blackened sky,
Pluck the rose that bleeds with wicked thorns,
For the sun is past zenith and twilight is nigh.

Gods, you will be hurt and bloody and bruised,
You'll float 'mongst the stars, sinking into the pitch,
Your body and mind may be beat and abused,
Yet you'll know the gamut of life, full and rich.

Take that plunge, take that leap of faith,
Thriving in both the pleasure and pain,
To not is to be but a wandering wraith,
So burn in the sunshine and dance in the rain.

BEAUTY MATTERS

Beauty is in the grit of life,
Where thorn freckled flowers are vibrant and rife,
It's in the coarse weeds and lush mud of the earth,
A gushing wellspring of deep magic and mirth.

Beauty will save us all,
Long after all around us has met the great fall,
Not always will it be so pretty in its wake,
Ah, but what it can give us and what it can take.

Beauty is a reviving light,
A flush and fervid fire in the coldest chasms of night,
Worthy of reverence in its dominant display,
For the diadem it wears is of the greatest array,
Flush with both terror and benevolent grace,
With a power so potent it cannot be effaced,
Wielding its might with both guile and gall,
And inspiring Man with its rapturous call,
Timeless and sacred as the paramount muse,
Yet what it can do for you, is for you to choose.

TUNNEL RAT

Deep beneath that jungle of war,
In the darkened bowels of the land,
Loyal foremost to the Corps,
Walks a wary soul with knife in hand,

It's black as pitch and silent too,
Yet he knows he's not alone,
He creeps his way stealthily through,
Struck by fear yet brave to the bone.

What horrors await him no man can say,
Will brothers and family see him again,
Will he once more know the light of day,
Will the war and the carnage ever end?

LIGHTNING IN A BOTTLE

Ephemeral is the flash of light that glimmers as it strikes,
Never to be seen again, for no two passings are alike,
But such fleeting moments make the day, and even more the mortal age,
For nothing lasts forever, as time and change exact their wage,

Sometimes the clouds do darken and there's lightning in the air,
A bolt of blazing beauty to be claimed by those who dare,
Sparking in its pulsing course yet evanescent in its fall,
The radiance of a second striking one with shock and awe,

A tender transient tryst in the sweet sultry swells of night,
Lovers locked in embrace beneath the soft and pale moonlight,
With whispers drifting on the breeze so fragile is their wake,
The love will be but memory by the time the day does break,

The iron band of brothers, found in the struggle and the mirth,
The friendship of a lifetime, priceless in its worth,
Yet paths of vision branch and break, leading blameless men apart,
Simply caught upon the tides of choice but still loyal in their hearts,

The timeless wisdom of your fathers and those stories that they told,
Shared around the glowing fire midst winter's biting cold,
A glimpse into the faded past or towards higher, hidden truths,
Knowledge to be given for the guiltless ignorance of youth,

A simple rolling journey, where the finish holds no sway,

Where friends can sit in silence, so comfortable are they,
Just grateful for the bond in which their presence brings some ease,
On an ageless trip of companionship where time slips like the breeze,

A gust of bursting laughter shared in company of friends,
Or the silent peace with family as the day comes to an end,
The briefest lulls of solace as you hold a baby tight,
Or speak with your aging father long into the night,

For every instant of great grandeur is a flashing bolt of light,
A passing gift of life that casts back the blackened night,
And every roaring blaze that bursts down from 'pon high,
May be captured in a glass while such beauty is nigh,

But even such a feat never secures a full gain,
For the glass may then break or roll fast down the lane,
As every moment you capture seems to long to disperse,
Like that bolt of bold brilliance striking the earth,

Thus that romance of night may be lost to the day,
And the friends you once knew may have gone their own ways,
As the stories you heard now do fade in their force,
Following your fathers in their own mortal course,

Yet for all of heaven's fire and the shards of clear glass,
And the fugacious moments that could not long last,
The striking magnificence of that sublime awe,
Still scorches a mark that's radiant and raw.

A LEAP OF FAITH

Into the sea I go,
Unsure of what awaits,
My heart I blindly bestow,
Leaving it all to the fates.

THE JUNGLE AND THE MOUNTAIN

Oh seeker of the highest peak,
Trekker of the clime,
What lofty summit do you seek,
In your quest for the sublime.

The path trails off and fades away,
You're now caught within the vine,
Shrouded from the light of day,
Without compass or guiding sign.

What else would you even ask for,
Is it not the untrammeled realm you sought,
A pristine scape for you to explore,
With land and beast to be fought.

Trailblazer, forger of the road,
With but the mount far off in sight,
And the jungle adding to your load,
In your tangled, valiant plight.

So break through the verdant wood,
There be vistas for which you long,
Where every climb tests manhood,
And every trail besets the strong.

Thus any rugged mount will do,

Many a climb is worth the dare,
But conquered only by the few,
Who think the journey's just as fair.

So seek those shining crowns,
For every peak reflects the sun,
But the jungle wrapping all around,
Is still a gauntlet to be won.

THE TOWER

Axis Mundi of a life, shattered 'cross the field,
Once a mighty monolith, the prize of lifeblood's yield,
A tower now but toppled, cruelly crumbled to the earth,
The fractured, ruined remnant of one's identity and worth,

Dust and devastation coldly claim the leaden land,
As stacks of stone lay scattered by god's heartless hand,
Heavy splintered blocks now sinking deep into the muck,
While wood and iron smoke from the tower thunder struck,

Worn and weathered tools sit rusting midst the wreck,
Their blades and bits now broken, their handles ashen flecked,
Crippled by their service in years of toil and abuse,
To render such a spire for it to be but utterly reduced,

And there before that mangled heap sits a spent and haggard man,
The weight of devastation crushing all his dreams and plans,
While calluses eclipse the flesh and tears threaten on the lash,
For an opus of the magnum class smote to dust and ash,

Yet time does tick and move and the clouds of fate do drift,
As a ray of silver sun slips through the hazy rift,
Thus the harried form lets a final solemn sigh,
And casts his head aback to glimpse the bright and dawning sky,

Then rising from his anguish, he steels his rugged jaw,

The fire of his spirit bursting through the abject pall,
As he grabs his broken tools and clears the ravaged plot,
Beginning once again and never speaking of his lot.

IN THE VEIL OF RAIN

Pink blossomed umbrella, with me and you beneath the rain,
I stand within your luscious bosom like a lustful, loving swain,
As the warm waters of the wind beat softly on the earthen floor,
The rich and mulchy undergrowth seeps up into my core.

DRIFTER

I drifted out on an open song,
And took the road both far and long,
To what hidden country I could not tell,
I was but caught up in the gypsy's spell.

SON OF HERMES

On wingèd foot I fly, striking naught but racing wind,
Harbinger of godly speed, ground beneath I cut and rend,
Over field of teeming gold, my feet move like the scythe,
Carving through the leafy growth of heavy, wooded life.

Dashing cross the mortal lands, outpacing steadfast fate,
Gliding over risk and ruin with fire blazing gait,
Like an arrow through the sunlit sky, soaring mad and free,
Bringer of the roaring storm, breaker of the sea.

Rapid like the thrusting spear, gleaming in the sun,
Maker of the bitter gales that rush behind me as I run,
Fleetly foot and lusty limb carry me through the day,
The tides of speed and victory hold me to the way.

VAGRANT YOUTH

Oh young man don't you know,
There are no rules where we're to go,
Just pack your bags and don't be long,
Adventure's singing its siren song.

Heed not the warnings of the old,
For mistakes you gain are gleaming gold,
Just take the step and clear the way,
Remember nothing is here to stay.

Oh young man how I envy you,
And yet it's pity that I feel too,
Free as the wind you drift along,
Yet lacking a place where you belong.

Follow where your soul does lead,
Yet know life is more than vagrancy,
So have your adventure and make it grand,
But freedom has its own demand.

FLIGHT OF THE DRAGONS

They fly aloft in shrouded cloud,
Or lurk below in unearthed ground,
Fiery beasts, avid and proud,
Guarding their glittering, bountiful mounds.

With rows of fangs and bellies of fire,
And bat like wings that cut the air,
Agents of null, both cunning and dire,
Come to wreak havoc and sow despair.

You squabble over petty feuds,
Tossed about on treacherous waves,
And chatter over fictitious news,
As the dragon comes to make you slaves.

The realm demands a stalwart knight,
With gleaming armor and gallant heart,
Immune to sickly, hysterical plight,
A man that stands a breed apart.

For the flight of the dragon is gaining height,
Spreading its fire across the land,
Demanding action from all faithful knights,
That charge the serpent with sword in hand.

MAN'S DOMINION

That which is fierce and that which is wild,
Those creatures that frighten, allure, and beguile,
Tis the labor of man to challenge the feral,
With the pleasure of conquest found deep in the peril.

From fast racing steeds that buck and rear,
And horned, hulking brutes that charge like a spear,
To goliaths of the jungle that stomp and thrash,
And armored skinned devils that strike in a flash.

There be humped ungulates that bellow and spit,
And poised feminine figures that refuse to submit,
Those paragons of the most deadly of game,
That man cannot help but to go forth and claim.

The hunt and the fray is his to fight and command,
The joy of the struggle won by cunning and hand,
To impose his will on the creatures of earth,
The charge of order bestowed upon him at birth.

Man wrestles and dances with the raw and untamed,
He rides and he fights and lays hold of his claim,
With rope and saddle and club and whip,
He dominates beasts with an iron grip.

Plying practised skill and honed finesse,
Or by brazen rush towards certain death,
He commands the feral with wild desire,
Tis the struggle, the game, the beast he admires.

OLD HANDS

Old leather, beaten and bruised,
Scarred and pock marked with sundry hues,
Weathered and gnarled from years of abuse,
Each blotch and blemish proud tokens of use.

Old leather, that bends and twists,
That wraps knotted fingers and hard clenched fists,
Bearing hot heat or frigid snow drifts,
Worn, faded hide that deftly persists.

Old leather, still hardy and tough,
Tempered by age, now calloused and rough,
Poise and form gained where youth was sloughed,
Sporting the marks of a life good enough.

THE SLEEPING TITAN

Wake me when you need me, till then I wait and sleep,
Dormant and hibernating in the long forgotten deep,
A relic of the past, of rugged days long gone,
Yet with inevitable return, as like the coming of the dawn.

Wake me when you need me, till then I toss and stir,
The ancient hands of fate are sharpening their spurs,
An instrument of providence, invoking dreaded ire,
Sparked from ashen embers as like a raging fire.

Wake me when you need me, strike the drums of war,
A need for strength and valor is banging at the door,

A catalytic weapon now charged to fiery form,
Thundering with fury as like the roaring storm.

Wake me when you need me, the time has come again,
When fateful calls are hearkened by red-blooded men,
Barbarians are at the gates, the city stands to fall,
Rising from my restless sleep, Man the ageless wall.

A SKY WITH EAGLES

When eagles soar in lofty flight,
Watchers of the ancient rite,
Displaying boldly vital might,
The dawn is sure to come.

FIRE: SUN INCARNATE

Praise be to the sun,

The sacred fire burns evermore,

Man the great keeper.

CREATURES OF THE FLESH

For is the flesh not good, not a sacred sculpt of clay?
Look how the muscles ripple, how they tense and they obey,
And oh but the joy of the fingers, to work and dance and play,
Instruments of the arms, sun-kissed by the day.

For the chest does heave with mighty breath,
As veins pulse wide, defiant to death,
And shoulders that bulge so broad is their breadth,
The heart roars out deep in the depths.

For legs that pump like pistons of war,
Guided by feet that stalk, walk or soar,
So quick does one dash across earthen floor,
As legs cry out, demanding "More!"

For self-yoked men, bronze and bull-necked,
Truly ample of arm and honed intellect,
Mind and body both they honor and respect,
He may look to the stars but the ground he must trek.

WINDS OF CHANGE

Born to the bitter winds of the north that dash 'mongst the trees and the hills,
Carried down to the coastal swamps, where the raw Atlantic spills,
But like lightning my time did flash and the gale whipped me up in its will,
And off I went to sunny lands where memories linger still,

And in that land of dust and sand, I found rich and fruitful soil,
An oasis where I stretched my limbs under the bounty of my toil,
But despite my fledgling roots, my ground the wind did roil,
Lifting me from upon the earth in sudden, ceaseless moil,

Off across the gaping deep, to nameless, ancient lands,
I wandered and I labored in darkened jungles and drifting sands,
But the winds were swift and sharp and the time slipped through my hands,
Returning to that smote of earth where natives roam in bands,

A gale whipped up and drove me out, towards sunny southern coasts,
And across that lush and teeming land I wandered like a banished ghost,
Till tempests strange and wild assigned me to my next novel post,
And back I was within the north, amongst my kindred, blooded host,

But the wind was strong and stirring, gathering its might,
And I knew now the breeze was shifting, for me to take my flight,
Back to the southern shores or overseas and out of sight,
What winds will blow, I do not know, but to go is my burden and delight.

SONG OF THE GLADE KING

In the murky, bracken depths,
Glides a stolid, stave of death,
With lurid eyes and armored skin,
Bane of man with a mirthless grin.

In the darkness and the gloom,
He lurks and waits, portending doom,
With cruel endurance and wicked guile,
Phantom of hate with crafty wiles.

Tranquil tyrant of the teeming glade,
Its gentle torpor but a masquerade,
With a gorging maw never glutted,
Draconic demon, black and cold-blooded.

Yet perhaps this devil of the shadowed reach,
Employs some virtues that it can teach,
For matchless does the beast endure,
And in its own tenacity it is sure.

Ageless has the monster thrived,
Through aeons of ease and grace deprived,
Persisting through the ruinous dim,
When so many others had met their end.

Whilst gliding midst the shifting streams,
It basks in the sunny sultry beams,
And prospers in the turbid waves,
Snatching many a foe to their graves.

Eater of serpents, scourge of the snake,
Leaving naught but the mirror of the sun in its wake,
Ruling its kingdom with immutable command,
For it is one and lasting with the land.

With a patience born of primeval plight,
And power deeper than muscular might,
Infused with wisdom behind vivid sight,
And force of violence in its lethal bite,
The king of the glade endures.

THE LORD OF THE EARTH CONTENT

The lord of the earth is passed on by,
Yet he sits with a smile and a gleaming eye,
No great serpents to slay, no stars to align,
Yet his work and his pride are never outshined.

WHERE THE FOREST SPEAKS

Oh, shaman of the forest grove,

What have you seen, what do you know,

Tell me, guide me with your wisdom trove,

For where am I supposed to go?

FLORIDA MORNING

Ephemeral mist
Smoking above the pale glade
Reflecting the dawn.

LUSTER IN THE LOST LANDS

Lo! The hills be bleak and black,
Tombstones of this ancient grave,
Deep within this foggy vale,
Twisted roots and dark magic rave.

All is dead within this land,
All is lost and spent,
Yet from the rugged, knotted east,
Gold of dawn gleams in its ascent.

For in the void of endless wood,
And across the jagged slope,
Burns the triumph of the immortal sun,
And it's lusty, boundless hope.

KEEPER OF THE SWARD

Tending field with weathered hand,
Steward of a wooded land,
Watchful on his grassy mount,
And all is well by his account.

He tracks the sun across the sky,
Gives praise and thanks each day alive,
Each season brings its needful tasks,
But a day of good work be all he asks.

A land quite small in the world at large,
Yet deep and rich the soil of his charge,
Bountiful crop inexhaustibly reaped,
And a joy for life in the man is steeped.

To the old watcher upon the hill,
Pious in his humble, abundant fill,
Loyal to life and to the land,
Which he gladly tends with weathered hand.

DESIGNED FOR DAMAGE

The shield is polished, the armor gleams,
Spotless, shiny and iridescently clean,
It hangs on the wall, 'bove the warmth of the hearth,
Safe and sound without blemish or mark.

Yet what good is a shield that has not taken a hit,
What good be your armor without proven grit,
Pretty and dazzling like a portrait hung high,
But without adversity for it to defy.

Down from the mantle claim your shield,
Don that crisp armor and step onto the field,
Mud and blood and scratch and dent,
These you'll face but you're not designed to be mint.

GO WEST YOUNG MAN

Go west young man, towards the setting sun,

Go west young man, till the day is won,

Go while the road is open and wide,

Go while youth gallops at your side.

LEGACY OF MAN

Down, down to the muddy floor,
Back to those dateless days of yore,
Naked save hide and matted hair,
With snarling visage and lurid stare.

By ax or by club or by calloused hand,
Feet bare on snow, forest floor or sand,
Hardened and wary yet dangerously bold,
One and wandering with the untamed road.

Amidst howling winds or searing heat,
Under darkened bough or torrential sleet,
Prowling 'cross dark and twisted lands,
Forever walks bloodstained man.

OUT THE GATE

Slavering maw, bloody and torn,
With wicked eyes alight in utter scorn,
Two tons of fur and meat and bone,
Hate filled and bristling, he bellows his moan.

The rope is taut, the hands are steady,
You squeeze your legs, nod that you're ready,
The door swings wide, the beast snorts and bucks,
You brace yet glide, this be the tell and the crux.

Seconds scream by and you bounce and you jolt,
The adrenaline strikes like a mad lightning bolt,
The bell rings blaring and you crash to the ground,
Hoofbeats and crowd cheers are the only sound,

Climbing the fence with your soul still alight,
You bask in the glory of your eight second fight.

NIGREDO

Into the Woods of mist and frost,

Into cold darkness, the land of the lost,

Alone in the night with a flame in the heart,

To lose yourself and your way is a delicate art.

ADVENT OF THE SUN

The father sat atop his throne, the void held his fervid gaze,
All around him darkness swirled, chaos reigned unfazed,
From will of fire and vision bright, back was the blackness cast,
And in its stead with molten gold, blazing Sol held fast,
The darkness swarmed around it, but could not breach its light,
A roaring flame of defiance, raging against the eternal night.

A GOLDEN AGE

A golden age upon us, when men will stake their claim,

Emboldened by their winning of wealth, women and fame,

When men revel in their strength and hold not back their tongues,

While women bask in beauty and nourish the budding young,

As tech and innovation uplift and excite,

Elevating all of both opulent ease and squalid plight,

Racing us across the stars to unknown and thrilling lands,

Granting us higher minds and greater skill of hand,

As food is grown right at home, nutritive and pure,

While sunlight and movement is the most effective cure,

And young men that go to fight will know that it's a need,

For that call to arms will only sound with proper care and heed,

When reverent art and masterly music seize the golden day,

Their purifying beauty shining out on full display,

With visionaries of structure allowed to take the reigns,

For blocks of grey and dullness they will not even entertain,

But will hold deferent conversation with the wise and distant past,

While looking to the future, ensuring the good alone will last,

A time when wrongs are righted and nature has its say,

Where all across the thriving land people laugh and children play,

And so in this age of gleaming sun and golden hope and will,

Those lovers of strength and beauty will have their flourishing fill.

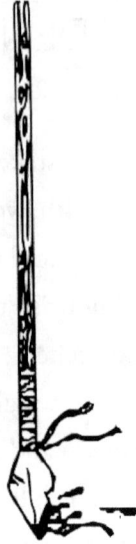

WAR

Lo! That sacred vehicle of glory,
When riches and renown are won,
With might of arm and manly valor,
That awesome violence is done,
Through the thrust of the spear,
By the slash of the sword,
Steely tendons choking life,
Claiming men across the sward,
Billowing chaos and strife,
That dominance they revel in,
Men standing atop their foes,
Sacking cities, razing homes,
Heedless of women and their pitiful woes,

Imbued with passion and love of the fight,
Snorting and charging like stallions untamed,
Rippling muscle and swiftness of foot,
Their manhood and honor raptly inflamed,
Red blooded men flaring with ardor,
Instruments of violent virtue and skill,
Men of pure substance, solid and staunch,
With unalloyed hearts of scorching iron-will.

DISILLUSIONMENT: A FALSE GOD

You've seen the sword splattered with blood,
And the sheen of youth slopped in mud,
Coffers of cowards filled to the brim,
And the heroic ideal fading in the dim,

The veils been lifted, the wool removed,
Fighting men broken, spent, and used,
The "good fight" festering like an ugly sore,
Hymns of glory and honor sung no more,

But do not let that thumos wane,
That desperate drive towards the heroic aim,
For that brilliant violence still holds sway,
When raw virility must claim the day,

Do not fade into that tepid dark,
But keep alight that flashing spark,
That torrid flame of manly might,
That burns and rages for epic fight,

For that fire in the heart of men,
That knows naught but conquest and the will to win,
Does strengthen limb and spur great deed,
Holding men loyal to that ancient creed,

An oath of life and manhood ablaze,

Beaming out from a lurid gaze,
That still holds glory as a lofty prize,
And knows that honor never dies.

REMNANTS OF WAR

Do not call me a hero for a hero I am not,
But you may call me a warrior, for war I have fought,
But now the war is far and gone, forgotten in the past,
And those who made it home again are counting out their last,
No longer youths with lusty eyes for glory of the field,
Nor eager grins and boisterous pride does heavy fighting yield,
Both boy and man they were, young men of a different time,
What was all it for? Those splendid youths lost in their prime,
Old and weathered relics now, tokens of the age,
And even I am now but a fading vestige of that rage,
For they were loyal to an oath, forsaken by their betters,
Yet treachery's not rewarded with bludgeons or iron fetters,
And so those breathless men, with immortal glory vowed,
Begin to wither in memory under Time's relentless shroud,
And so the old do venture to join their fellows in the dim,
Faithful warriors waning without their deathless song or hymn.

THE VISAGE OF HOMER

There for the first time I glimpsed him,
Just a flickering silhouette in the dim,
I had heard but whispers of his name,
But now, like Keats, felt for the first, his reign.

There in the shadows watching over his own,
Sat Homer quietly in the arms of his throne,
Beyond the wool of our eyes that clouded our sight,
Yet still alive and flaming with vigor and might.

The Homeric world, raw and untamed,
Casting our quaintness into a shadow of shame,
Yet Homer stands still, like an ageless portal,
Bedrock of our lives, naked and mortal.

WINTER MORNING

A white swathed land with bursting pink skies,
Jagged hilltops blooming with heavenly fire,
Flecked with hoary growth in their wintry guise,
Flaring canvas of the earth in its seasonal ire.

WHAT IS GOOD?

The night was cold and dark,
As a lone pilgrim made his way,
Till on the hill he gazed a spark,
Hearing minstrels sing and play,

A chorus of revelry broke the night,
As he wandered to the door,
Basked suddenly in golden light,
As he stepped onto the floor,

All around men drank and sang,

While barmaids served and laughed,
Music roared with strums and bangs,
And beer flowed freely from their drafts,

The room swayed like a joyous sea,
The whole building like a flame,
That raged against the bitter night that be,
Striving for its claim,

In the corner sat a hulking brute,
His face stern save for a grin,
Naked but naught for fur and loot,
A display of strong arm and bronze skin,

The bards did dance, singing his name,
As women fawned, stroking his chest
While praises were sung to his heroic fame,
Telling of trials and of daring quests,

To this towering figure, the pilgrim made,
Pushing through the carousing crowd,
Greeting the man of adventure and blade,
With request of audience, he bowed,

With a lightsome smile the brute gave a nod,
Speak ol wanderer and we'll hear your claim,
His voice stilling the room like that of a god,
The pilgrim then straightened and told why he came,

Oh great champion of this mortal plane,
I beseech you for wisdom to the riddles of life,

What is good, what is worthy, for what should one strain,
In such a fleeting existence of confusion and strife,

The barbarian laughed and tossed back his head,
Oh wayfarer tis an easy one indeed,
What is good is alive, what is bad is dead,
Good is the strong and the power of speed,

Great is the touch of a luscious lady,
No worse is a flagon full of mead,
A yes, a no, but never a maybe,
Are the only two words you'll ever need,

Redeeming are the virtues of beauty,
And there be beauty throughout the land,
Women with grace and men of duty,
That would defend it in heroic last stands,

Righteous is a fire for its raging light,
Glorious is the burn of the heavenly sun,
Joy be the victor's in a hard-won fight,
Or the exhaustion after a ripping run,

Cherished is a swaddled newborn.
But so too is the conquered foe,
For on both many an oath are sworn,
By which affinity and faith do grow,

Unrivaled, adventure reigns,
And those acts of ardent gall,
Whether climbing mounts or crossing plains,

Inspiring are they all,

Laughter is good, so too is food,
But better yet if they're combined,
For festivities will enhance the mood,
With a few glasses from the drink of the vine,

But hear me so, as there's more to learn,
Gods and monsters too are a boon,
For monsters always hold a treasure to earn,
And gods light the night like the moon,

Music is sweet and so too is art,
Matched with fighting and violence of arm,
For both will alight your mortal heart,
And both can deliver you from terrible harm,

Great is a hound striding at your side,
Not a better companion there be,
But equal to the dog is the horse you ride,
And not many other unions work with three,

While every innocent youngling is worthy,
And is it not so, for aren't they all,
But the plight of cruel men yields no mercy,
It is better the quicker they fall,

The fruit of the field should be wanted,
A grand harvest in every sphere,
As the farmer deserves to be vaunted,
His crop the source of much life and cheer,

But why oh wanderer do you wonder so,
About the easiest questions there be,
Ask a child and he will know,
Or a fisherman adrift at sea,

What is good is alive and pushing its bounds,
What is worthy is but a choice,
You can strive for peace or bloody crowns,
But when asking out loud, you'll hear only your voice,

Thus the barbarian spoke,
Taking a swig of his hearty ale,
But the pilgrim only tightened his cloak,
Then bowed and muttered a hail,

Then the figure swam through the crowd,
Disappearing out the night veiled door,
And the barbarian but laughed aloud,
And the room again began to roar.

THE WRATH OF ARISTODEMUS

Three-hundred men marched to the gate,
Not a man but one returned,
Rallying the warriors with hot-tempered hate,
Their spirits now roused, roared and burned,

The call rang out to every man of able arm,
Every sword and spear wrested from its perch,
Awakened cities blared out their alarms,
Heavy gates slamming shut with a lurch,

The hammer of blacksmiths blazed in the dim,
Lamentations of women swelled with fear,
Heavy shields held steady with brawny limb,
While gods turned away from supplication and prayer,

A thunderous quake rose from the veil,
The black shrouded throng loomed near,
Tearing over the land like a mighty dark gale,
Men were cut down with women running in fear,

But like crashing waves on the soulless shore,
They fell against the walls of men,
Spilling libations of blood and gore,
As screams pierced the deafening din,

Here stood the host of that honor bound land,

Defying that barbaric horde,
With a stalwart and loyal fighting band,
Foreign blood splattered 'cross the sward,

Across the plains and rugged hills,
Over the rolling pitch of the sea,
War raged on, a contest of wills,
Till home land was reclaimed and free,

Back to their haunt the enemy fled,
As the victors sang and gave cheer,
Never in vain was heroic blood bled,
For they held their land by courage and spear.

THE HAVEN OF CAMARADERIE

Outside the winter winds howl and bite,
In a starless land of perpetual night,
A vacant span of darkness and fright,
Where desperately life struggles and fights,

Yet within the glowing abode of man,
Gathered in company revels the clan,
Joined by warmth and selfless hand,
In this haven 'mongst bitter lands.

AGNI

Priest of the first men, an ikon of flame,
A light in the darkness, the giver of names,
Bane of the serpent from that yawning lair,
Idol of champions and great dragon slayers.

Cutting its lines across the land,
Where the perimeter stands tightly manned,
Guarding within the riches of life,
From draconic whispers of chaos and strife.

Roaring does it tell of higher aims,
Guiding men of the earth towards illustrious claims,
Herald of the sun of which all men rejoice,
A crier of virtue with a blazing voice.

Primordial paragon lighting the way,
Carrying the banner of blinding day,
Eternal emblem emblazoned in man,
As a light in obscure and darkened lands.

Primarch of flame spearheading the fight,
For a single torch blazing can cast back the night,
Raging against the serpents of the deep,
For Man and the light, this it will keep.

THE HEROIC AGE IS NOW

Oh fortunate one, born in a heroic age,
Brimming with bravery and righteous rage,
The sun beaming over you with golden rays,
Heralding the glory of coming days,

The gates are open, the path is paved,
Lady Luck's smiling on ventures braved,
Pick up your arms and don your cloak,
The time is golden, a bursting yolk,

Lift up your head and with your eyes behold,
Ringing out through the land is the call of the bold,
Under the flare of dawn, with promise and praise,
For those dauntless dynamos whose souls are ablaze,

Like golden youth, yours are the heights,
To gain and grow and to love and to fight,
Conquering and claiming the spoils of life,
An age of opportunity radiantly rife.

STEWARD OF THE HILLS

Grey-maned man of ashen hills,
Steward of a cloistered land,
Where the wind does bite in icy chills,
And ancient growth does grimly stand.

Amongst the leaden hills he walks,
Tending to his trust,
Keeper of the wild flocks,
Always doing what he must.

Alone amongst that faded wood,
Yet never solitary in soul,
Lord of earth both strong and good,
Holding vigil 'top his cherished knoll.

BE THE LIGHT

If the sky above is imbued with gray,
And a cloak of cloud covers the light of day,
If winter creeps in and forces it's stay,
Make it your task to be a luminous ray,

If darkness looms and threatens its reign,
And the light around you begins to wane,
Tap into your own like a gleaming gold vein,
And cast back all the gloom, the misery, and pain,

If the world is battered with rain and snow,
Then be the light setting yourself aglow,
Spouting out heat like a flashing flambeau,
A rousing force gushing an inexhaustible flow,

In a world where the light is covered or pale,
Towards the gloom and the darkness you must assail,
A lone beacon of light burning through the veil,
Make yourself the sun and dare to prevail.

THE VALUE OF A TREE

What is the value of a single tree,
One nondescript within a verdant sea,
Unassuming and average in degree,
But with lofty dreams of what it could be,

It could be a grand cabin with its grain on display,
Sitting high in the glade under full light of day,
Home to a family where children grow and play,
Set apart from the common, tree-laden array,

It could be the work of the finest of taste,
Perhaps an opulent table garnished with lace,
Or a reliquary with remnants so piously placed,
Or a humble church pew quietly graced,

It could serve as a handle for a hammer long worn,
Or the barrel of a pen with which vows are sworn,
It could be a grand casket for which kinfolk do mourn,
Or the cozy crib guarding a precious newborn,

A single tree strives and stretches for the sky,
It's aim is lofty and noble and high,
But woodsmen never come with their trade to ply,
And it never grows higher than its fellows nearby,

It never became a table or chair,

Nor the holy addition to a house of prayer,
Never a home filled with love and care,
Or a tiny cradle guarding a baby so fair,

It doesn't lament nor cast off the blame,
But neither does it feel the weight of shame,
It looks inside at the mighty tree it became,
Still fruitful and imposing without any acclaim,

How is the value of a single tree weighed,
Does it come from its growth or the fruit it has made,
Or the use of its lumber as a rank accolade,
Or perhaps the stretch of its limbs and it's offer of shade,

The worth of a tree is not so plain,
It's simply a tree on a peculiar campaign,
Common in wood but growing unique in grain,
With value so indefinite it's hard to ascertain.

TO BE A MAN

To be strong without needing to flash your might,

Knowing when to run and when to fight,

To push on with resolve and grit,

Knowing when to charge ahead and knowing when to quit,

To let your actions speak for you,

Filled with pride but a modesty too,

To take many a risk both daring and bold,

Yet wise and discerning, never needing extolled,

To never lose that inner flame,

But never for itself, seeking fame,

To be youthful in spirit but old in soul,

Knowing both those two have their proper role,

To keep honor and duty as guiding lights,

Keeping feet on the ground and eyes towards the heights,

To suffer great loss and failure too,

But taking it in stride as you see yourself through,

To be a man of higher aim,

Yet knowing you and other men are one in the same,

To never abandon that heroic touch,

But knowing that instinct can oft be too much,

To give it your all in all that you've done,

Seeing your wins and your losses, feeling proud of each one,

To live life to the fullest and blaze bright like the sun,

Knowing when it's your time your regrets will be none.

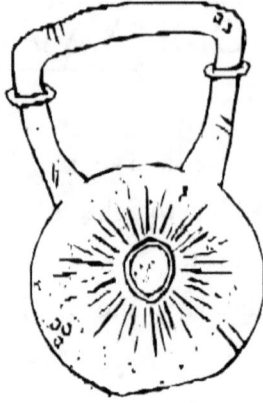

CULT OF THE FLESH

Glistening skin against the warm kiss of day,
Bronzed muscle flexing sculpted like clay,
To the temple of iron the pious venture to pray,
Loyal to virtue and the hard earned way.

Disciples trekking the righteous road,
Where beauty and strength find their abode,
Where glory is gleaned from a heavy load,
And footprints still flicker where hero's once strode.

Toward the heights of might and thus that of life,
Reveling in the path of sublime strife,
That burns like the forging of a well tempered knife,
For a devotion where honor and merit are rife,

With eyes towards the sky, feet firmly on the earth,

The exertion of strength the source of homage and mirth,

Thus vigor and passion one's tokens of worth,

Wrought from a life of corporeal birth.

NOTHING IS OVER

Nothing is over for him who will try,
There be no end till that final goodbye,
For man is only as finished as he feels,
As brittle as glass or as hardy as steel.

PLIGHT OF THE ROLLING STONE

A rolling stone caught in the descent,

Rolling on and on in discontent,

With no solid ground on which to orient,

Rolling on and on despite its dissent.

THE BRICK

A lone brick is not much at all,
Hard and strong but does not make a wall,
Easy to step over, easy to throw,
Unable to stop the slightest of blows,

Quickly it's buried under the grass,
Or tossed like refuse in a motley mass,
What good is a brick all on its own,
Just a weight, a block, an obtrusive stone,

But a brick in a wall is bolstered and raised,
Withstanding mighty blows firm and unfazed,
Each brick a link distinct yet concerted,
The strength of the wall plainly asserted,

For the strength of the wall is in every block,
But a brick on its own is but idle stock,
To be joined with the wall in unified might,
Or cast alone to the side to suffer its blight.

NOW I AM BECOME SPEED

I feel the sun caress my skin,
Emboldened by its light,
Merging with the racing wind,
As Hermes grants me flight,

Across rolling hills I fly,
Through fields of gold I dash,
Forth-most host of speed am I,
Here and gone in a flash,

My lungs billow full and surge,
Legs of fire pump and churn,
From maelstrom of speed I emerge,
Body singing against the burn.

The world around me falls away,
Nothing left but me and my deed,
Boldly blazing under light of day,
Now I am become speed.

UNDER CRIMSON SUNS
AND DANCING PETALS

Gunman of the western plains,
With a big iron at his side,
Riding hard through his domain,
Of single mind and hawk-eyed,

The town rises up before him,
The sun hangs heavy overhead,
As buzzards circle slow and grim,
Patient for the dead,

The man steps off from his steed,
As he gazes at the blazing sun,
His fingers flex and he feels their speed,
As they long for the weight of the gun,

Into the center of town he strides,
To face his baneful foe,
Today he lives or dies,
But only god above does know,

Far across the misty seas,
A man strolls slowly into town,
A sword hangs past his knees,
As he bears a brooding frown,

The streets of dirt run clear,
Not a soul is in the midst,
Til a man afar decides to dare,
Reaching for the handle by his wrist,

Swords are drawn as words are spared,
The two men march to meet their fate,
With prayers long said they are prepared,
Their ancestors watch and wait,

Back on the dusty road,
Beneath that high noon sun,
They'll reap what they have sown,
The two men of the gun,

Time slips by in silence,
Holstered is their steel,
As hands are set for violence,
Their souls ignite with zeal,

Heavy burns the arid heat,
Sweat trickles down their backs,
Tension clouds the empty street,
They stand poised for the attack,

Now within that distant land,
The men of the blade advance,
Their steel held deftly in their hands,
As they begin their sanguine dance,

Stolid is their rugged cast,
Yet lurid eyes alight with fire,
Each man himself, bold and vast,
Wielding cold and tempered ire,

Lightning flashes through the air,
Metal duels with hardy mettle,
Both blades vying in ruthless flair,
Blood dripping like sakura petals,

The gunslingers hold their breath,
Only their hearts do drum and beat,
Till a flare of fire summons death,
So quick were the men in the street,

Smoke billows from the barrel,

As the hawk-eyed man inhales,
Delivered again from mortal peril,
For the speed of his draw prevailed,

Now a body lies limp in the dust,
With deep crimson coating the ground,
The buzzards descend in a gust,
As the victor rides out of town,

The swordsmen wage war in the east,
Death sparking from vicious steel,
Like a melee of savage beasts,
The bloodlust is all they feel,

Till the brooding man makes his mark,
As his weapon finds vital skin,
The eyes of his foe grow dark,
For the final thrust is driven in,

Now a figure lies foul and inert,
Its weary soul adrift on the breeze,
As bright petals drop to the dirt,
The victor fades off to the trees,

Warrior of the western span,
Fighter of the eastern sphere,
Paragons of martial Man,
To the way of sword and gun they adhere.

TIDES OF CHANGE

The man stood before the river,
Thinking back across the years,
The roaring waters had shifted,
As they had every time he was here.
When he was but a boy,
he had waded in the stream,
So carefree and blissful,
But things were not as they had seemed,
When he emerged from the waters,
He was now a plucky youth,
With a taste for adventure and trouble,
And a stirring interest in women to boot,
But as he stepped back in the waters,
On a scorching summer's day,
He found himself quite taller,
Finally a young man here to stay,
But the bugles of war did bellow,
And he left for quite an age,
And the waters flowed on and on,
Til he came back battered and enraged,
He thought to cool his head,
As he dipped into the pool,
And the heat of the bitter fighting,
Began to soothe and cool,
Then he strode out from the waters,
And found himself a wife,

Abandoned to the romance,
And the thrilling love of life,
He brought his wife to the river,
And together they did swim,
And when they stepped up on the shore,
There was a little boy like him,
And through the years they'd visit,
Always swimming in the waves,
But as the waters roared,
He realized there was nothing he could save,
For his boy went in the river,
And out he came a man,
And he and his wife too,
Had changed in quite a span,
And the waters roared on and on,
And often the man came by,
Each time the river was different,
And the man thought so too am I,
And now he stood before the river,
Long in the tooth and grey of mane,
But he smiled at the rushing currents,
And into the waters he stepped again.

FORLORN GLORY

They were boys that wanted glory,
And to prove that they were men,
To have their names in song and story,
For they could return with honor then.

Each boy a rifle bestowed,
Each told only half a truth,
Towards immortal glory they strode,
Unbeknownst at the cost of their youth.

So full of hope, so full of life,
Before they bravely faced the fire,
Then straight into the den of strife,
Immolated on sacred pyre.

They were boys and they were men,
But romantics each and every one
As much warriors as the best of them,
Doing what men have always done.

For they were boys that wanted glory,
And to prove that they were men,
But now their young and blooming story,
Has come to bitter end.

THE HORSEMAN ARRIVES

The drums of war begin to beat, far off in distant lands,

The men are marching with their arms steady in their hands,

The cloak of fear has settled, heavy on the streets,

Your little girl comes asking if there's food enough to eat,

The neighbors boy is far and gone, readied with a gun,

You hear the roar of aeroplanes that blacken out the sun,

The womenfolk lamenting, shrouded in their veils,

And all the homes around are boarded up with nails,

The rider of the pale horse answered quickly to the call,

You hunker in your home, plagued by the horror of it all.

MOONLIGHT

The full moon hangs high,
Tonight I am not alone,
It carries the light.

THE WAY

The path is narrow and never ending,

Rugged and lonely and ever ascending,

You must have strength and you must have grit,

You must be courageous and never lose your wit,

The gods of the way will demand their share,

You'll sacrifice and obey or you best not even dare,

For many a man will stumble from the way,

While many will surrender and wander away,

Many cold nights will gnaw at your mind,

You'll look back and wonder at the road behind,

Many days you'll struggle, you'll slip and you'll fall,

Doubt will creep in but it is then you must crawl,

You will struggle and suffer and fail many a day,

But never abandon the path, never stray from the way.

PERSEVERANCE

Many defeats you will face on the field of life,

Over and over again you shall face hardship and strife,

But defeat is not destiny and failure's not fate,

Seven times down, yet up counts eight.

BE YOUR OWN HERO

You've failed, you've failed and you've failed again,
You've forsaken your gods and all your kinsmen,
What supplications now could you offer them,
What libations could you pour to absolve your sins,
What gestures of atonement could you possibly extend,
What purification must be sought to correct and amend,
Damn you man, failure is not fate,
You can start again now, be reborn, why wait,
Set yourself alight and push back the night,
Not absorbed by the pitch but a raging, roaring light,
Melt yourself down to nothing but cinder,
Carry your own ashes through the cold of winter,
To the mountaintop you go with the vessel of your soul,
Now man, now, you must be your own hero!

FIGHT ON!

Rage man, rage against the whispers of death,
Strive, struggle and fight with your dying breath!
If they try for you, leave them bloody and bent,
Only go if you must when your strength is spent,
You have life in you yet, still a man of sheer will,
March on, fight on, let them know you live still!

MATURATION

The master and the student walked side by side,

Amongst bamboo groves that stretched sky high,

The silence was heavy in the cool morning air,

Till the student bursted forth to say his share,

Master I've listened to all that you've said,

But it's true I have some ideas in my head,

The master's brow raised but he let the boy speak,

He nodded to the youth, a smile pushing at his cheek,

All this focus and temperance of which you expound,

Does hem all my strength of which I am proud,

My aggression, my passion, you mean to lock it away,

Channel your anger is what you always say,

But just as my sword can grow dull with age,

So too would my spirit if suppressed in a cage,

Why should I temper my warlike soul,

To end up like the weak, feeble and old,

Look at my strength and the might of youth,

Unsheathing his sword, he hacked at the shoots,

Several stalks splintered, shattered and bent,

A mass of stems hanging gnarled and limp,

Look oh master at the force I do wield,

Why slacken my will, why demand my youth yield,

The old master nodded, his face weathered yet kind,

He thought for a moment as if searching his mind,

Young man I understand where you're coming from,

You think age and maturity will make you tame and numb,

But maturation is not the abating of will,

It is a honing, an increase, a waxing of skill,

A sword must be tempered to produce its keen blade,

Just so a man forged can be polished or frayed,

You lose not the strength nor the spirit of man,

But channel it, cultivate it to be at your command,

Then like lightning in a raging gale,

The masters sword was drawn, arching through the pale,

A single slice as quick as the wind,

And several walls of bamboo stood severed on end,

The old master sighed, sheathing his sword,

As silence fell again across the grassy sward,

The youth dropped his gaze and said not a word,

As master and student resumed their walk through the wood.

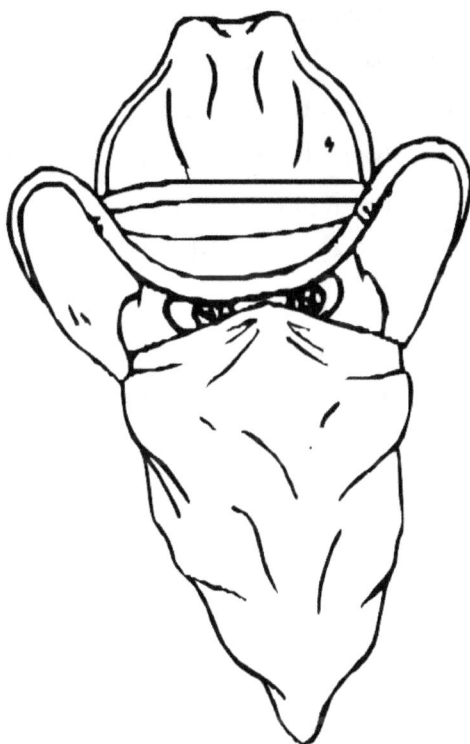

LEAD AND WHISKEY

The scent of whisky on the breath,
Riding hard towards certain death,
The flash of steel beneath the sun,
Drawing out his heavy gun,
Horses grunt, lathered in sweat,
One man against six, a losing bet,
Dauntless he charges into the foe,
Barrage of fire, smoke billows,
The shouts of men assail the air,

As cries of shock turn to swears,
Over bloody ground the men regroup,
Three men short of the baleful troop,
The lonesome rider turns back towards the fray,
His fate before him, to live or die on this day,
Another charge, another spur of his steed,
He lets loose a cry as he gains in his speed,
Shots start to crack and rip through the air,
A grin breaks his face under a thousand yard stare,
A final clash with destiny, a final strike at death,
Pounding heart, steady hands, and whisky on the breath.

IF THE WORLD IS DARK

If the world is dark and shrouded,
And the skies are bleak and clouded,
With the wind both cold and biting,
And the shadows deep and frightening,
In lands both bare and broken,
With not a joy thus spoken,
Build a fire in the dark.

If women weep and children hurt,
And able men lay down inert,
As the toll of pain covers the day,
Under a sky both dead and grey,
With every ailment and every ache,
That never softens and never slakes,
Carry the fire through the night.

If the sun is hidden in the gloom,
And criers shriek portending doom,
As serpents slither in the mists,
Beneath the feet of hedonists,
While wingèd beasts take to the skies,
With shadows looming, spreading lies,
Rise up like the blazing sun.

If men grow limp and the days grow dark,
In that blackness strike a spark,

Let not the serpents have their way,
Usher forth a blinding day,
That casts back the darkness from the land,
As you rage and burn where you stand,
Light the fire, carry the light,
become the sun in a world of night.

A GAZE LIFTED

Pilgrim on a darkened road,
Your head is weary, hanging low,
Your back is bent from heavy load,
Lost and dejected with nowhere to go,
You search for answers never found,
And cry out to dead and nameless gods,
Crossing soulless forsaken ground,
With yourself and the world at fervent odds,
How long can you wander through ashen land?
How long must the struggle endure?
You have the strength to barely stand?
The whisper of the void now has an allure.

But oh weary pilgrim if you just lifted your head,
Letting the shadows fall away,
An alluvion of sun would pour into their stead,
For so illustrious is the bright light of day,
Seek not so much truth but the lucid and clear,
The light spreads like a beneficent balm,
Casting away all your pain and fear,
Or reminding you of a power both vital and calm,
Heralding the rise of your heroic dawn,
Blazes forth the glory of that god,
Enlivening you with both spirit and brawn,
Till life is now a load that you zealously laud.

PRAISE THE SUN

Grand undying Sun,
Glorious in your power,
Homage unto thee.

HOSPITALITY

Do not devour the cattle of the sun,
You must pay obeisance to the golden one,
Respect his station and obey his laws,
For you walk in his fields and luminous halls,

For want of his warmth and elucidating light,
You've ventured from home and far outta sight,
To be taken in in your vagabond plight,
Begging for food and a room for the night,

Genial and generous presides your host,
Yet all parties involved must comply with their posts,
Remember your manners and offer no slight,
For the practice of Xenia's an inviolable rite.

THE JOY OF AN APPLE

The sweetness of an apple with a crisp crunch,
Juicy and savory as you think and you munch,
Simply enjoying the taste as you work out a hunch,
Or contemplate life with your humble red lunch.

THE RETURN OF THE LICH

The lich lurks down in its darkened haunt,
Waiting to exact it's unwavering want,
To extinguish all life in it's icy embrace,
With its wretched and vile, inverted grace,

But a hero arises in his burgeoning youth,
To slash at the tongue of vehement truth,
Defiant in the face of mortal decimation,
That whispers honeyed words of total negation,

Into the lair of the lich he strides,
Armed with naught but courage and the sword at his side,
Down into the darkness of Stygian gloom,
To confront once again that herald of doom,

Like all great heroes have done once before,
To forever defy the immortal threat at the door,
His will glowing and blazing with red-blooded vim,
Like a torch in the empty and fathomless dim,

Through the hordes of fiends he deftly crusades,
Towards the heart of darkness and the home of hades,
Where the looming lich dwells in his baleful guile,
To meet this new hero in his definitive trial,

In the blackest pit he finds him, the lightless lich,

Whispering spells in an attempt to bewitch,
But the brazen hero charges, utterly unfazed,
As his sword bursts alight like searing sun-rays,

Metal meets bone in a crackling clang,
Beneath the hero's cries and the lich's black pangs,
On his mettle the hero stormed and strove,
Rending and cleaving, back the lich he drove,

Down in that den of darkness and death,
A pitched battle was waged for Man's sacred breath,
With the terror of the lich cresting with hate,
And the hero forestalling Man's inevitable Fate,

Till the final blow was struck with a piercing thrust,
And the lich quietly sank and turned into dust,
His body of rot now lost to the day,
Vanquished by the hero triumphant in the fray,

Now the battle is won and the age is saved,
By that plucky young hero who so valiantly braved,
Into the lair of that loathsome lich,
Slaying the foe in that feverous pitch,

Yet the soul of the lich has scattered and spread,
Dispersed into it's totems of nocuous dread,
To be challenged once again in a distant span,
By a valiant young hero with the spirit of Man.

THE SIREN SONG OF MAN

Wise men may know of the folly of youth,
It's raging passion, it's thumotic drive,
That lead men astray in its camouflaged truth,
For which they so desperately and valiantly strive,

A great many men are gripped by it's pledge,
To be given honor and glory so golden and rife,
If only they dare and step off from that ledge,
To be consumed by that fire of immortal life,

A promise kept without its gilded trim,
For the dead pay no heed to life-giving light,
Devoured by the truth naked and dim,
For their glorious moment of heroic plight,

Yet what greater love can there be for a man,
An eagle 'mongst men in prodigious flight,
Than to lay down his life for brother and land,
His name sung forever in the hymns of the fight,

To stand fast alone 'midst that clamorous fray,
Vast and defiant in his fated campaign,
Exacting renown in the heroic display,
Where the heights of high valor are deftly attained,

He may know the cause a deceptive ploy,

That devious men craft self-seeking schemes,
But that the warrior heart is of a different alloy,
Made of honor, brotherhood, and high heroic dreams,

For life may be cheap and the gambits galore,
In a world where the wool has been shorn,
But the path of the warrior prevails prime at its core,
Where the mantle of merit remains proudly adorned.

DOMINANCE

Man versus man in a battle of death,
Bodies locked in the fateful fray,
Covered in sweat and dripping blood,
Like wild beasts over slaughtered prey,

Limbs of iron bludgeon and strike,
Heavy bones splinter and crack,
Biting and bashing in utter rage,
Vying for primacy in savage attack,

They roll on the ground, grunting with hate,
Their eyes glowing like a ghastly flame,
Hands grasping for that breath filled neck,
As a lion bites the throat of its game,

Sweat stings the sight, breath is labored and short,
They slip with the blood in their grips,
A rib is cracked and a nose is shattered,
As red mottled slaver sprays from their lips,

Filled with naught but desperate hate,
Only the din of the melee sounds,
And the drive to live and to conquer,
On these primal blood soaked grounds,

Muscles surge with pumping blood,

Sinew snaps like the crack of the sky,
Nostrils flare above gritted teeth,
Under the lurid burn of their eyes,

Until a victor claims the life,
Of that breathless beast within the dirt,
The body limp and dreadfully maimed,
Forever broken and inert,

Now standing proud above his claim,
That champion of tooth and claw,
Revels in his gruesome winnings,
And the fortune of that ancient law,

His body marred and deeply bruised,
As blood cloaks him in its spate,
But exuberant is that dominant man,
Who won that calloused hand of fate,

Filled with life and virile mirth,
Atop the body of his beaten foe,
Claiming wealth and triumph,
Taking his woman in her woe,

That man conquering man,
Unmatched in prowess and might,
Superior in his station,
Gained by the violence of the fight.

PITILESS BEASTS

Self-pity is it now, that shrouds you in its cloak,
A dejected lamenting of your own sorry lot,
But are you not a bull, strong and self-yoked,
Your blood coursing with life and boiling hot,

Why do you sit there in your troubles and woes,
Oh so you've stumbled and strayed off the track,
Your towers have crumbled while besieged by foes,
And the sky hangs heavy in a curtain of black,

But look at yourself and see that bull of a man,
With both might and mind to endure and win,
Not destined for defeat holding fate in your hands,
No matter the failure, the loss, or the sin,

For not a bird of the air that fell dead to the ground,
Or a roaming cur frozen gaunt in the snow,
Ever once shed a tear or let a whimpering sound,
As it suffered and died in life-wrenching woe.

ROAD GODS

Chariot of steel ripping across the land,
Rolling and racing guided by your hand,
Moving like a spirit of lightning speed,
Commanding your numinous mechanical steed,

Churning violently over plain and hill,
Swept up in the clip of the pumping thrill,
Faster than the lords of the bygone age,
With your screaming engine of combusting rage,

Driver and mount molded into one,
Pistons throbbing like billowing lungs,
Rubber screeching over blackened street,
As you fuse with the vessel in your dashing feat,

It's chassis glinting 'gainst the brilliant sun,
Shooting by like the shot of a mighty gun,
As the wind rips past you in envious spite,
Vying for primacy 'gainst your dazzling flight,

You hold steady the wheel in your skillful grasp,
Forcing the pedal under its laborious gasp,
As you soar like a god across the mortal plane,
Exuberant and vast in your driving reign.

GREY MAN VERSUS THE HERO

But a shade amongst the living, you boast no mark or sign,
Befitting a stouthearted hero in his hale and hardy prime,
Swathed in grey and faceless you move about the throng,
A blank and vapid visage, not a figure brave and strong,

Under the mantle of anonymity, you sport the inane gray,
Afraid to show your colors or face the challenges of day,
Like a recluse rife with tremor forced to leave his hidden haunt,
An anxious agoraphobe, to seem benign, his greatest want,

Contrasted by the figure who flies his standard proud,
A man of gravitas contemptuous of the shroud,
Who dares to tread the world both vivid and ablaze,
Knowing he's a symbol, guiding in his ways,

Like an icon of the upper realm, an embodiment of valor,
His bearing of the hero, his mere presence potent power,
Inspiring in his carriage, giving rise to emulation,
Emboldening those around to climb above their station,

Not haughty nor pretentious, nor intolerably vain,
But the demeanor of a nobody he would never deign,
To wear just as the lowly in want to fade away,
But rather look and be a hero, not a man of lifeless gray.

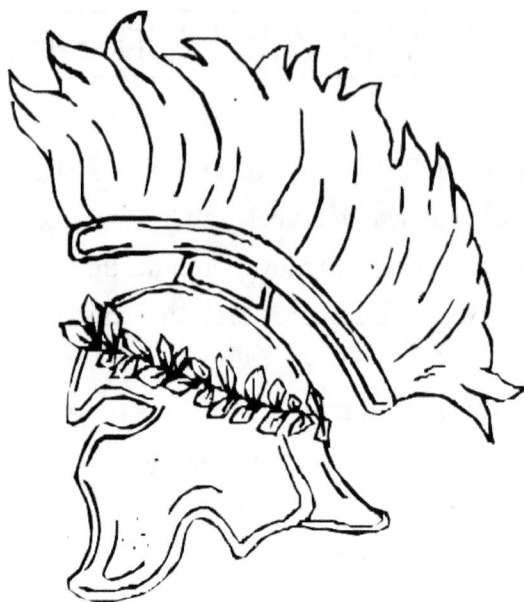

ARISTEIA

Full grown yet youthful lion of the field,
Rending foreign foe who refuses to yield,
Your quick brazen limbs spattered with blood,
As you break and you trample the enemy to the mud,

Your rage sings out in its deathless song,
While all around you gathers the threat of the throng,
Encircling you in its forbidding grip,
With flashing sword blades and gleaming spear tips,

Your chest heaves high and your eyes glow alight,
An element of wrath at home in the fight,

Your body is poised, beaming bold and vast,
As you hear the hymns of aristeia extolling your last,

In your bloody wake a grove of men are felled,
Their dark looming limbs all but withheld,
As they slash and they tear at your radiant flesh,
Ensnaring you in their deathly, ironclad mesh,

The mercurial gods look on in stolid assent,
With no enchantments of luck nor arms that augment,
But left to the fates to sentence the man,
Who still holds his destiny in his own willful hands,

While limbs are swiftly severed as blood is spilt and gushing,
Droves of the enemy lay slain in their rushing,
Towards you, that mighty man of deftly arm,
Whose valiant deed seems to guard you from mortal harm,

Yet for every man claimed in your merciless haste,
Another score of the horde charges 'cross that crimson waste,
That besiege and assail you on all compassed sides,
Hacking and cleaving in relentless strides,

And in your glorious moment of godlike grace,
Despite the skill of your violence and the drive of your pace,
Your golden moment, your zenith, has hellaciously dawned,
The sun waxing and waning for your glory just beyond,

Till a spear finds its mark in the meat of your thigh,
And a sword slices deep, rupturing your eye,
Your body is bludgeoned, your flesh is torn,

As blood sprays out like a bursting sea-storm,

Yet still in your defiance and beastly purge,
You roar and you rage under the hostile surge,
Till your head is severed and your eyes no longer glow,
Cut down by the swords of the swarming foe,

Now the breath of life has left you and your body's but a husk,
Your glory rising like the dawn as your spirit drifts into the dusk,
For your name will live on in triumphant song,
Praising the deeds of a man so courageous and strong,

Your aristeia will ascend to the heroic heights,
Men will honor your feats in sacred, pious rites,
For immortal you shall be in deed and name,
Your body but bones but your glory bursting aflame.

THE VALUE OF A STAR

Although there be a million stars up in the ebon sky,

Each single mote does twinkle and capture the enchanted eye,

And though one star may fade and dim, drifting into dark,

The sky becomes a little colder without that scintillating spark,

So every star does have a name, and an orbit of its own,

A gravitational pull so that that star is never alone,

And so It glows and gleams driving back that Stygian gloom,

As it's warmth and heat are felt as a bright and nourishing boon,

Some stars are vivid and bright, some but a distant flickering flame,

But each star in its essence is practically the same,

And so if you take a single star out from the canvass of the night,

The world will be a little darker without its warm and shining light.

LIFE IS MYTH

Is not your life a lusty legend, a mighty monolithic myth,
A seminal story singing out with you the progenitor and protagonist,

Born to blaze like a burning beacon beaming 'gainst the baneful black,
A blooded bull bellowing that no bitter bonds can keep back,

Bestowed at birth a blaring fate both fortunate and fertile,
And a numinous noteworthy name if one but accepts the trial,

Piously plunging into life, peeling apart the plating,
Proudly producing a personal myth in your own poetical creating,

Is not who you are and what you do the making of a myth,
With meaning in every mark you make like some robust and rugged
romanticist,

An aiming adherent of adventure and ardent acolyte of ambition,
To but voice your vim and vigor and create a myth of your own volition,

To live a tale of plenty and in your destiny dare to dream,
For your life is imbued with meaning for those who hold myth in high
esteem.

POLARIS

Fire fixed within the dark,
High above a flaring spark,
Glaring out so cold and stark,
Dominant Polaris,

Guiding like an austere light,
Beacon of the aimless plight,
Lantern of the shapeless night,
Illustrious Polaris,

Gemstone of the sunless sky,
Godly In it's realm on high,
Watchful as the world spins by,
Imperishable Polaris.

LEFT BEHIND

The men are marching off to war and all the boys lament,
Left behind to agonize in their desperate discontent,
Eager to be off to fight and prove their manly worth,
Afraid to miss their fleeting chance upon that martial earth,

Heedless of the elders and all their wary wit,
Enraptured were they all by those men in soldier's kit,
Engrossed in all the stories of their fathers and their wars,
With a single dream to join those renowned and righteous corps,

Thus left behind there's not but shame to keep the sullen youth,
And not a word does mollify regardless of its truth,
For a boy in want to earn his name and prove his mettle true,
Peace is but a blighting curse upon those fiery few,

Yet now they're spared from such a fate of the ruined and the dead,
Perhaps for some the tract of war is destined to be tread.

THE GUISE OF NIHILISM

You masquerade as wisdom and proclaim the greatest truths,
"But dust and ash we are," is a claim difficult to refute,
Legacy is worthless and glory is for fools,
And not a thing be given meaning, is the strictest of all rules,

We're here then gone and when we're dead, It won't matter anyway,
Nothing worthy's left in your stead, and nothing is here to stay,
Strength is in acceptance and surrender breeds the wise,
This is just your life, absent purpose and lacking prize,

Once mighty men and reigning champs now speak of empty gain,
For nothing will be remembered and life is spent in vain,
You'll be dead and gone, and rot away, forsaken by the gods,
But they don't exist anyway, they're just beliefs for chumps and clods,

But damn you don't you see, you are the bane of utter life,
And though it's "truth" you speak, your hands hold the bloody knife,
That severs all connection to both the world and to the soul,
And leaves you naught but empty in a barren, vapid lull,

Delusional I am not, might be your stoic quip,
But it is delusion that you serve, in the "reality" you grip,
It simply is what it is, I'm just a realist you might say,
But that be a weary lie leading others far astray,

Hubris it be for you think you have the truth,

And so certain that you are you'll bash the dreams of youth,
That dare to live with strength and hope in visions grand,
Willing to risk it all and find a hill on which to stand,

You claim this is the way, you've found life on sunless roads,
That this overturning "truth" has reduced your mortal load,
Though it all seems but a cope, or at least a lack of wit,
With no creative force to pull you from the listless pit,

For this "wisdom" that you spout only shows the starting mark,
While your outlook is still lightless so impoverished by the dark,
Yet there be a greater light shining farther up the trail,
For back you've pulled one curtain but there hangs another veil.

FLAMMA: THE VICTORIOUS

Fearless flame fond of the fight,
Hero of the marble pit,
Breaking men in that gruesome rite,
Renowned for your guts and grit,

A score of men and fourteen more,
Did dare to seize your head,
As nine were stalled plus a loss of four,
But twenty one counted were dead,

Your warring reign carried you to age,
Four offers of freedom denied,
Loyal to the fight and your bloody stage,
A champion immured yet deified,

A warrior by will but a slave by dictum,
And the choice to be a victor, never a victim.

PUSHING WEST

When destiny did drive them west,
And the trail was open to the bold,
Eastrons left their urban nests,
To make their claim for land and gold,

Men of the horse and gritty gun,
Matchless In their dauntless deeds,
Save for those men who also won,
That westward tract of desperate need,

For that barkeep and that rugged clerk,
Or that man of plow and blacksmith too,
All braved the trials and never shirked,
From their strife or what they swore to do,

All humble men without a name,
Yet Men they were all the same.

GILES COREY: THE GUILTLESS

Fear and corruption tinge the dark Salem air,
As warlocks and witches gallivant in nightmares,
The townsfolk are panicked, the officials debased,
Roused into a frenzy in their punitive chase,

Every man is a suspect, every woman in doubt,
Judgement looms grimly for both wicked and devout,
Torn from their homes and stripped to the skin,
To extract their confessions and purify their sins,

Till a man of the plow, made of granite and grit,
Is brought into question with no hope to acquit,
But is coerced to confess and offer a plea,
Or face retribution of the Lord Almighty,

Refusing to yield and bow to the crowd,
Firm in his faith he stands upright and proud,
To defy the demand for his judicial claim,
So to hold to his estate, his principles, and name,

Brought to the court to pry out his offense,
And forced bare to the ground without penitence,
To be pressed with great stones till out rang his plea,
When verdict could be meted by sacral decree,

But the weight of the stones did pile and swell,

And still the righteous suspect refused to yell,
Or even usher a whisper of his criminal case,
As he laid in the dirt in his implacable brace,

More and more, the stones stacked on his broken bulk,
While around him the townsfolk but gaped and gawked,
Till the stones could go no more and the question arose,
"Will you now plead for your life or continue to oppose?"

But the man laid silent and his eyes burned ablaze,
And cranking his neck met the constables gaze,
Resolved in his purpose and resolute in his fate,
Defiant to the last he but cried out "More weight!"

THE SEA-BIRD

Soaring ever beyond the pale,
Crooning in its lonesome flight,
Calling men to raise their sails,
To brave the brine and test their might,

Perched atop the flotsam lorn,
Elusive as a phantom keel,
It's song a dirge in which it mourns,
For those that chase with lusty zeal,

Skimming atop that darkened deep,
Like an emblem of opportunity,
For men who take that daring leap,
And cast it all upon the sea,

Calling above that rippling wake,
It sadly sings for the sailor's sake.

ODE TO THE SNIPERS

Men of the dreadful long gun, those stalkers in the shade,
Like revenants of the reaper in their shrouded ambuscade,
Preying on those heedless men that dare to bare their head,
Wraiths of war and lightning that unleash their bolts of lead,

In their wild suits they wander like wolves upon the prowl,
The single echo of their shot their only prideful howl,
Ravenous in their action yet patient in their post,
Haunting fields of carnage like lycanthropic ghosts,

With martial skill they ply their trade, matchless in their art,
Hardened hunters of the heath set a breed apart,
Silent in their suffering as they cull the mortal flock,
Wardens of the felling grounds, keepers of the stalk.

HOMER'S CONTEST

That burning envy of the soul that billows and enflames,
Igniting that driving passion towards higher minded aims,
Possessed by jealous spirit when in the presence of a better,
And a galvanizing impulse to burst apart your fetters,

You look about and see a man of greater strength or speed,
And now the ambitious upset becomes a hungry, fervent need,
You take to weights or to the track with a single minded end,
And in your avid rivalry both you and your foe ascend,

Or you glimpse a man of lofty mind, with works by clever hands,
And you relish in the action that this suddenly demands,
The specter of competition now racing through your veins,
Forcing out your budding greatness in hot and fervid strains,

Artist versus artist in a duel of creative deed,
Beggar versus beggar in a match of desperate need,
Athlete versus athlete in a bout of bodily feat,
Farmer versus farmer in a reap of golden wheat,

The joy of competition raging hot throughout the fold,
Eluding lowly station by a spurring of the bold,
Rising to the challenge and dueling with the greats,
Never to extinguish but to best or emulate,

Like iron sharpens iron, this demand upon your trade,
To step into that honing ring of which the dare is made,
Striving ever upward 'gainst the sources of your greed,
To win or lose with dauntless tries while daring to exceed.

AGELESS ODYSSEY

Lo! Oh man of twists and turns how I've know your winding fate,
For I, myself have lived in that never ending spate,
Lost amongst the waves of that unharvestable sea,
At the mercy of the gods in their implacable decrees,

Then washed ashore on nameless lands where danger beset me so,
Until I had fully realized what I'd been cruelly sent there to know,
Voluptuous vixens and sensuous sirens assailed me at every turn,
While massive monsters besieged me against that which I did yearn,

To return to hearth and home and to the place of my respite,
Where my blood and land awaited me in a different kind of plight,
To finally claim that elusive want and leave the past at sea,
A man of many twists and turns, polytropon I be.

BROTHER IN ARMS

In the foxhole I found him, brother in my fight,
Us alone in the world, in our grim and hellish plight,
The night was deep and broken by the bedlam of the gun,
While our prayers were desperate and silent, pleading for the sun,

The earth was torn and shattered as we watched warily from our pit,
Just my brother and I together with nothing but our grit,
For the night was dark and deadly but for the flashing of the fire,
That ripped and tore through the air in unabated ire,

I saw him in the shadows, the visage of my kin,
A brother in the truest sense, beget by virile men,
And I felt a tear roll down my cheek for I knew of no greater bond,
Than that between all fighting men in this time and beyond.

THE HERO AND THE MAN

I set out to be a warrior, a man of might and arm,
Bewitched by the tantalizing crooning of the sirens luscious charm,
Following in that path of that heroic breaker of men,
Single eyed in my pursuit to stride into that iron-din,

But in my youthful callowness and my eager pledge to Mars,
The fates had not foretold my place amongst the stars,
And thus for me the war eluded, dashing all my hope,
Like a chariot split asunder broken free from its rope,

I set out to be a warrior, but it was war I never made,
And for all my aspirations, there were other gods to which I prayed,
To walk the warrior way still harbors my adherence,
And now the path I walk is one of twofold perseverance,

With pen and sword I make my mark, flourishing my muse,
While the man of many twists and turns, into me that ideal was infused,
An all encompassing man, with still the glory of life and light,
A man who is plenty more but still a warrior of the fight.

THE LABOR OF CREATION

A mountain was in labor shaking all the earth,
A titan of the land in its desperate pangs of birth,
Roaring in its struggle to beget a piece of worth,
But for all its grievous quakings came but a meager dearth,

For from the rubble sprang a mouse, tiny and unfit,
Not the spawn of muses in their sublime, sacred writ,
But the product of exertion in a herculean fit,
And the honest toil of a mind full of avid wit,

Just a minute mouse it was, from the ether it was freed,
And any bounty yielded serves a great and mortal need,
For fruit enough the mountain bore in its hellacious deed,
And still painful is the process that produces but a seed,

For the quivers of creation may split the muddled mount,
In its daring to extract greatness from the fount,
And though it's scanty produce is of such a small amount,
Its creative act alone is an admirable account.

TANK MAN: THE TITAN OF TIANANMEN

Nineteen Eighty Nine and the Orients aflame,
The tyrannical regime is the rancid source of blame,
With its corruption and its censors like an iron boot,
It's domineering power rotten to the root,

The killing and the slaughter has swept across the land,
Butchering brave souls who would defiantly stand,
As men march in lockstep to fire upon those few,
And tanks roll to the square pushing to get through,

Screaming rips across the air as terror is dispensed,
The forceful arm of government has yet to be stood against,
Over bodies churn the tracks of the faceless prowling tanks,
Straight towards the heart of protesters in their desperate ranks,

A final sweep of arm to clear up this nasty mess,
To silence all the upset and exterminate the pests,
To seize control again and squash the harsh dissent,
An easy feat to gain with the dreadful tanks advent,

Down the road they roar into the bloodied square,
Unopposed and certain in their cold and metal glare,
Till suddenly and with a squeal the lead comes to a halt,
The entire convoy jolting, dead in their assault,

Now in the middle of the road stands a lone and daring man,

Headed home from market with bags still in his hands,
A day set out for errands not marked for fearless feat,
Yet here he was, courage spurred and standing in the street,

No battle cry or rites goodbye did fix him for his fate,
While fear sat upon him like a dark and heavy weight,
But here he was determined and his courage rose and grew,
Not a man born a hero, just a man knowing what to do,

A lone man, he blocks the tanks, like a Spartan at the gates,
Resolute and steady in his righteous, mortal straits,
No route around realize the tanks as they begin to make a plea,
But the bold man won't have it and refuses to agree,

Atop the tank he clambers, bags still in his hands,
Forcefully asserting his peoples fair demands,
And the commander of the tank bows his head in shame,
Before this manly spirit and his just and noble claim,

Upon the tank he stands like a graven statue aglow,
Basked in blinding golden light like a hero of long ago,
Proudly and defiantly in a valorous spur to act,
Answering the call and stopping tanks in their tracks,

Nineteen Eighty Nine and the Orients afire,
The country is in chaos and the situation's dire,
But a lone man appears to defy that cruel command,
All because he chose to act with bags still in his hands.

ETHEREAL MISTS

Misty morning fog
Billowing above the glade
Lucid veil of dawn
A phantom world so fleeting
'Mongst titans of Spanish moss.

JOHN HENRY: THE STEEL-DRIVING MAN

Mountain of a man born with the mighty hammer in his hand,
Driving steel and breaking stone across the sweeping land,
Brawny as a bristling bull filled with fire in his chest,
Not afraid to stake his name in herculean contest,

Working in the scorching heat and the frigid winds of winter,
He drove the nails and smote the rocks until they cracked and splintered,
Steel driving man he was, cutting paths of track and rail,
Too full of pride and virile vim to ever slack or fail,

Engines churned and smokestacks billowed 'cross all the lines he laid,
So masterful John Henry was at his rough but relished trade,

Both company and crew alike stood amazed at such a man,
Relentless in his efforts, he stood like a titan fierce and grand,

Until one hot and scorching day the tracks began to quiver,
With the advent of the drill machine and its future to deliver,
A mechanistic monster come to dominate the field,
It's produce far superior than a single man could yield,

Thus the working men but sighed and shook their heads dismayed,
For here stood the metal harbinger to take their jobs away,
No man could match its might they cried or keep its speedy pace,
Yet stepping forth John Henry roared let's test that in a race,

Awestruck were the men at the gall of such a dare,
As the drill machine rolled forward with its wicked hardware,
Before the wall of rock it now waited for its foe,
As John Henry with his hammer poised for the starting blow,

Then deathly silence fell upon the tense and nervous crowd,
John Henry standing like a statue, motionless and proud,
The drill machine growling like a beast within its cage,
Both adversaries brimming with single-minded rage,

The starting gun went off resounding in the hush,
As the crack of splitting rock erupted in the rush,
Man against machine embattled in the toil,
John Henry dripping sweat, the drill bleeding blackened oil,

Through the rock they burrowed, dust fogging up the view,
Machine and man both smothered in their effort to push through,
Buried in the tunnel, drill howled and hammer clanged,

A din of metal booming with every mighty mallet bang,

Fire flew from every blow, like Hephaestus at the forge,
While the drill machine bucked and belched, utterly engorged,
Darkness swam around them, powder smothered like a pall,
Both driving blindly with their steel to break through the stygian wall,

Shards of rock assailed the air, lashing at skin and steel,
While John Henry felt his muscles burn, his flesh urging him to kneel,
As the drill machine but pulled ahead, vying for the win,
John Henry bowed his heavy head, disheartened and chagrined,

While In the darkness and dusty gloom, John Henry staggered on,
The roar of the drill machine, taunting his failing brawn,
His chest did heave and labor as sweat flooded down his back,
His body and mind both succumbing to the tunnel's baneful black,

Yet as he stumbled on, nearly broken and all but beat,
A resolve arose within his heart that knew not of dark defeat,
For in that bleak and sunless hollow, John Henry found a light,
A fire flowing through his veins burning for the fight,

With hard and heavy hammer he renewed his grave assault,
Bursting through the gnarled stone of that deep and dreaded vault,
Like pistons did his muscles pump, his sinew like snapping steel,
A colossus of might and conviction, relentless in the ordeal,

His hammer sparked with wicked flame as he thundered through the dim,
Smoke billowed from his steely sledge while steam rose above his skin,
Like molten lava his mallet burned, so ferocious was his charge,
The specter of destruction looming grim and large,

So fiercely did John Henry drive he caught the dour drill,
A battle of boiling rage, cold machine against blazing will,
Now pressing the attack, the two fought like gods of war,
Their field of battle crumbling the further that they bored,

Breath and steam did surge, merging with the veil of dust,
Both man and machine alike threatening to combust,
So laborious was their chore that pain and mayhem soared,
Feverish and desperate to reach the grassy sward,

Now enraptured in the struggle, the contenders blazed and fumed,
Till a bright and blinding light burst through the earthen tomb,
With a volcanic force of might John Henry hammered ahead,
Breaking through the wall, soaked in sweat and sanguine red,

A chorus of cheers split the air as the crowd beheld the man,
Standing on that grassy sward with the hammer in his hand,
While the drill machine but bellowed now busting through the rock,
Its bolts and gears now cracking from the strain and brutal shock,

But all eyes were on John Henry for in his triumph he did fall,
That mountain of a man collapsed in a morbid sprawl,
For so determined was his drive and so daring was his deed,
His heart had burst asunder in his effort to succeed,

Yet in the ensuing woe and in the shadow of his act,
That hero of will and steel left a legacy on those tracks,
For that body of John Henry though exhausted and interred,
Bore a bold and deathless spirit that could never be deterred.

AVATAR OF THE STORM

Thunder from the sky,
I walk this mortal domain,
Wielding the lightning.

THE MUSE OF CIVILIZATION

Marred in sweat and dirt, their bodies lithe and lean,
Like wolves they roved the badlands with morals lurid and obscene,
They relished in the hunt with crude and savage arm,
Strangers to the garden and the culture granting farm,

Blood dripping from their bearded maws, beneath eyes of baleful fire,
They fought against their kindred own, hearts filled with scathing ire,
For conquest of the feeble foe and violence of club and rod,
They worshiped at their alters, serving them as cruel and gluttonous gods,

They knew no art or industry, their trade the stalk and war,
Wrapped within their meager trappings of matted fur and gore,
Prowling 'mongst their squalid huts they kept but dirt and rock,
No letters bled through paper sheets nor numbers counting stock,

This lot of theirs, they relished in and knew no other way,
But the womenfolk were dainty and inspiring in their sway,
So soft and tender was their flesh, so radiant their charm,
How beautiful they were and so vulnerable to harm,

Wood and stone soon gathered to make a mighty wall,
As hearths in homes were glutted with the fruitage of the maw,
Furrows of the field soon interlaced the land,
While spade replaced the spear in once deft and dauntless hands,

Woven wool and linen now replaced the ragged hide,

While once bloody hands now glistened, from fabric freshly dyed,
With the florid script of scholarship now keeping full account,
For the burgeoning bureaucracy now became the paramount,

Canvas bled with color, sporting vivid sublime scenes,
That hung upon the walls above rich gourmet cuisines,
While instruments of song did fill the comely halls,
And the women of the house sauntered 'round like pampered dolls,

Yet the loveliness of woman still drove the visionaries on,
To but impress the fairer sex with more than brazen brawn,
Erecting looming monoliths that glimmered in the day,
Or sculpting marble mannequins and painted pots of clay,

Songs of love and triumph resounded smoothly in the air,
As men of poetry and music strived to win their tenderhearted share,
And if the urbane arts could not purchase one a dame,
Then surely could the winning of wealth and widespread fame,

Competing for great power or status noble and renowned,
Men invented and created in their effort to astound,
Cities sprung like wild flowers and flourished in their flush,
As the race for feminine affection reached a mad and torrid rush,

For man can do without and can thrive in savage lands,
With but the clothes on his back and what he carries in his hands,
But the feminine so dainty needed pleased and protected,
And in this the deed was done, for it was civilization man erected.

FEAR PREDOMINANT

Primeval god of the dark unknown,
Wielding dominion from its unrivaled throne,
Inexorable arbiter of man's valorous will,
Either condemning his life or granting its fill,

Deathless guide steering stouthearted souls,
Forever detested and never extolled,
Yet generous to those who answer its call,
Men who don't cower but respond with firm gall,

Restless daemon that feeds on all men,
Torturing the craven with what could have been,
Gnawing away at a man's lusty life,
Till he's not but a shell filled with regret and strife,

Acknowledged as a savior yet offered no praise,
Intimate of Man since black bygone days,
When Man first crawled out of that primordial muck,
And with both courage and caution was duly struck,

Immortal element both a blessing and a blight,
Lurking in Man and his inner recesses of night,
To be heeded when needed but often challenged outright,
For with discernment and daring Man may ascend to great heights.

NOBODY MAKES IT OUT ALIVE

First rule of reality, nobody makes it out alive,
Everyone struggles and everyone dies,
But so what, who cares, life is cheap,
Fate is cruel and what you sow, you reap,

Get over yourself and your myopic view,
Everyone has something and that's nothing new,
Life is serious but it ain't that deep,
Every man in history has had reason to weep,

But mistake me not there's no cynicism here,
And realisms a lie that's nothing but drear,
Existence is what it is, don't expect more,
But at the same time there's grandeur galore,

Life is beautiful not a bitter imposition,
It's just reality is raw, part of the human condition.

LIVE DANGEROUSLY

Whatever trails you tread in life and visions for which you aim,
They must spur you on towards greatness and set your heart aflame,
They must challenge you and test your will and threaten your very life,
For strength and growth shall not be found in a lack of striving strife,

Your path will wind and weave and the goal may shift or shatter,
But if you dared in dire deed that's all that really matters,
If you learned the world and made yourself towards the image of your ideal,
If greater virtue was wrought from you, it was worth the trying ordeal,

You must seek the roads that demand of you an increase of your mettle,
And those that acquaint you gravely with your faculties of fiery fettle,
For once you forsake the dangerous way for the certainty of the secure,
You'll unman your very being and cast away your virile vigor.

DAWN OF THE FATHER

Immortal void with boundless reach,
Empty and silent holding absolute reign,
Till an emergent warrior pushed in through the breach,
Bringing both light and oblivion's bane,

Casting back that blackened blight,
The void shrank and withered from the fray,
Smote by the storm and the lucent light,
That the warrior brought with the dawning day,

Ascendant now the warrior won,
His sharp gaze sweeping his fertile fief,
With blazing light beamed forth the sun,
The warrior now the pater-chief,

Yet restless lurks that void of none,
And The Fathers work is never done.

A FIGHTING MAN

A fighting man you were born to be,
why forsake your destiny,
son of man thoroughbred,
you walk the path your fathers led,

Through darkened tunnels you may roam,
And countless seas far off from home,
Trudging mountains in the snow,
In lonely lands you do not know,

Meeting monsters in your quest,
And beaten down without a rest,
Yet rising steady every time,
Drenched in sweat and bloody grime,

Fearful not of pain and death,
For in you flows eternal breath,
Carrying you to lofty halls,
Where immortal brothers stand the walls,

Hard is the road you walk upon,
Yet blazing always like the dawn,
You rage against that bitter black,
No matter the load upon your back,

Deathless does your spirit soar,

A man of storm and savage war,
Contented in that messy strife,
High upon that peak of life.

TITANS OF IRON AND EARTH

Metallurgical mammoths roaming the face of the earth,
Shaping the land to their purpose and extracting plutonian worth,
Surging with fire and fuel, they labor weariless in the day,
Roars erupting from iron stomachs smeared with dirt and clay,

Beasts of burden bellowing like behemoths of brutish war,
Ravaging wood and plain in their quest for opulent ore,
Instruments of steely might plying their terrestrial trade,
Challenging the power of nature on their proud colossal crusade,

Glorious in their dominion of both fertile field and bog,
Mountains bow before them while skies turn black with smog,
Laborious is their yoke set in their herculean chore,
Roving the land like titans from merciless days of yore.

THE BATTLE OF CAMARÓN

Sixty-five men of foreign birth sworn to the fealty of France,
Determined to hold their honor 'gainst the three thousand Mexican
advance,
Ensconced in the hacienda, the men of the Legion prepared,
Captain Danjou on wooden hand, till victory or death he declared,

Bottles of wine were passed around, final words fore the fight were spoke,
Grave was the deed before the men, the honor of the Legion invoked,
"Surrender." Said the dire dispatch, or face the bloody scourge,
We've plenty of lead Danjou began, and we just might yet emerge,

Promptly came the Mexican host, thunderously charging the fort,
Cries of men soon rent the air as defenders fired out from their ports,
Waves of men rushed the walls breaking like the sea on the shore,
Felled by the flurry of the Legion who was no stranger to bloodshed or war,

Repulsed was the encroaching throng, turned back to but rally anew,
Though bereft were the legionaries, for lifeless laid Captain Danjou,
Sorrowful stood those loyal men yet rage soon gleamed in their eyes,
Remembering their oath and their honor they each braced for their own
demise,

Onward again the Mexicans came, unleashing the fury of hell,
Screaming rounds ripping the din, men falling 'neath the shot and the shell,
Cries of anguish ruptured throats dry from the heat of the day,
Bodies choking the gorging ground, glutted by the blood of the fray,

Another appeal for surrender came offered to the Legion's best,
Though but twenty remained, the legionaries never deigned to accept the request,
Suddenly their stout stronghold did take to the flame and blazed,
Seeking shelter in the stable the legionaries watched as their bastion was razed,

Again came the roar of the guns, bombarding the few that remained,
Naught but five of the Legion stood defiantly alive and unmaimed,
Ammunition exhausted they boldly stood marred in the blood and the sweat,
Resolutely they heeded the order to forthrightly "fix bayonets!",

Bursting out of the stables, the five men of the Legion drove,
Gunfire quickly erupted, before the lieutenant a legionnaire dove,
Riddled with bullets his body lay, cut down in his selfless act,
While the Mexican army rallied, preparing for their final attack,

Surrounded now upon every side, only three of the men held on,
Steeling themselves for the fatal charge bayonets were once more drawn,
Accept defeat the enemy cried or you'll be slaughtered like pigs and sheep,
On one condition the legionaries said, save our men and our arms we'll keep,

Covered in carnage and swathed by blood the field of the battle grew still,
Fidelity and honor of the Legion kept by their strength of will,
Tenacious were those legionaries, like demons in the fearful fray,
Yet men of the Legion they were, keeping both oath and honor that day.

THE CURRENT YOU CHOOSE

At the crossroads once again, where the nexus twists as trellis,
An interwoven seascape for all the rushing streams,
Knowing deluge and drought in their enigmatic currents,
Carrying a man to ruin or his highest hopes and dreams,

Every current charges, relentless in its course,
Insensitive to men who stand upon the shore,
Fearful of the rapids and the murky, morose mist,
Unwilling to find out what it is he lives for,

Yet every stream does wind and weave, leading out to sea,
And every river races with grave and grievous waves,
While a man who longs to sail must get his footing wet,
Risking all to ride the swells on the current that he braves,

For often it is said that all rivers lead to sea,
And not a single river is "right" save the one you decide to be.

A BEAUTIFUL LIE AND AN UGLY TRUTH

Young men may yearn for the glory of war,
Thumotic hearts pumping with heroic ardor,
Strong and courageous, with selfless aim,
Exemplars of manhood in hallowed halls of fame,

Old men may know of the horrors of war,
Now given to peace, asking what it all was for,
Condemning the plight of the warrior way,
Their experience of bloodshed holding ultimate sway,

Foredoomed struggles and valiant last stands,
Are both repugnantly wretched and gloriously grand,
Both an ugly truth and a beautiful lie,
For which many gallant souls so willing die,

Forever extolled upon those lofty heights,
Both dreadfully dark and blazingly bright,
Worthy of praise in its manful fall,
Yet there's other ways to reach immortal halls.

INTO THE BREACH

Into the breach once more,
Have faith and heart my friends,
This is but love and war,
And a life worth fighting for.

THE CALL OF THE KÓRYOS

Red-blooded youth, full of vigor and vim,
Your eyes lurid with fire as you skulk through the dim,
That darkness calling you, towards an unknown end,
A primal voice compelling you to fight and contend,

To race with the wind and disappear with the sun,
Brash bane of the realm in your nightly runs,
Alongside those boys of your warlike band,
Enraptured in youth as you ravage the land,

With an ardent heart you chase every whim,
While life pumping muscles bulge from your limbs,
As a craving, a need, wells up from within,
To howl at the moon, wrapped in lupine skin,

Restless and bold, you long for a fight,
'Gainst a fearsome force of the dark, dreaded night,
For which you can slay and assert your claim,
To earn high renown for your station and name,

You must hearken the call while the iron is hot,
And dangerously dare for destiny is wrought,
Touching the earth and tending your flame,
Forever a beast, proud and untamed.

ETERNAL YOUTH

The setting Sun of youth, need not take your flame,
Fine is the passage of time, but abdication the source of shame,
A body may be worn but muscle need not soften,
For a sloven man steps early to a foul and squalid coffin,

A brilliant mind may dull and lose its lustrous sheen,
Like a well-used blade of yore, not as sleek and not as keen,
Yet it's edge may still be lethal, more formidable for the skill,
Wielded by the man with a death-defying will,

Miles may mount and tax the flesh, even more so the bludgeoned soul,
And inevitable pain does come to exact its mortal toll,
Yet a man of stalwart stock, may keep his youthful grace,
An inexplicable quality, that age cannot erase,

The longing for adventure, the faith in ideals high,
That love for land and body, that only the weak and craven deny,
To exercise one's might and dare in deeds of dread,
To love and fight and dream in a vibrant life well led,

Relentless is the flow of time and the breath of life may wan,
Mind and body may weaken and age brings ample change,
But eternal is the soul of youth if in naught but blazing spirit,
And this be the crux of the aging man, for his virtue and his merit.

IT AIN'T THAT DEEP

Whatever your problem,
It ain't that deep,
And whatever your mountains,
They aren't that steep,

Any darkness that you're in,
Cannot withstand the light,
Any load upon your back,
Cannot restrain your might,

The fear within your heart,
Cannot touch your burning soul,
The worry in your head,
But a distraction from your goal,

The weariness you feel,
Is but a lack of aim,
The confidence you lack,
From unnecessary shame,

Just live your life,
But that means you must live,
A life that you value,
That's all there is.

SUNSHOWERS

Life is messy, but beautiful,
A muddy, moiling crucible,
With no great truth or reason,
Just the ever-changing season,
Where showers fall with rays,
In both stormy sunny days,
Or blizzards hold great splendor,
With tiny flakes so tender,
Where winds may whip and bite,
As a force of awesome might,
And lucid skies do glow
Down on icy lands below,
For life is such a storm,
At once a varied form,
With all its snow and rain,
A mix of gaiety and pain,
And with all its Sun and sorrow,
The climate shifting with each morrow.

THE HARVEST

Once more over the top,
Across the harrowed field,
Cut down like golden crop,
Husks left in the sanguine slop.

STORM UPON THE SEA

Dark clouds cloak the sea,
Far upon that night veiled main,
More lightning than rain,
Beautiful and blistering,
Bolts of thunder shake the deep.

THE BRIGHT

It is a good day to die,
The sun shines immortal overhead,
I ready myself for another try,
It is a good day to die.

DEPLETED SOUL

If into obscurity I do pass, into that blackened void of none,
Nameless and anonymous, when my life is limp and done,
Let me not lament, for that life that I have wrought,
But close my eyes in peace, for the yield that I begot,

For if my soul was spent, and my faculties were drained,
No matter of their laurels, my work was not in vain,
And as long as no great surplus, was on the table left,
Then it was a life well lived, and my mark was still impressed,

And rather I would have, my mind and body worn,
Than confront my final days, with potential left forlorn,
For regardless of acclaim, man's life is one created,
Until his soul is empty and his life is fully sated.

VIOLENCE IS GOLDEN

A man unacquainted with violence can hardly call himself a man,
For he cannot protect his own, so behind others he must stand,
Convinced the world could be peaceful, ignoring the reality of life,
Yet always relying on others to wield the sanctioned gun or knife,

For every law threatens violence, and every foundation of fiat is force,
And any man not dangerous, is simply having his violence outsourced,
While peaceful he may think himself, violence is done on his behalf,
Like a pacifistic monk permitted, and protected by men of civic wrath,

Not the only answer is violence, but always the final answer it be,
Beneath every glittering law and every couth and highbrowed decree,
Innate in man is violence, to which all peoples are beholden,
That ultimate mark of currency, indelible and golden.

MARCH OF THE INFANTRY

Here comes the march of infantry, hands eager on their guns,
Raising hell across the land like Are's bastard sons,
Voracious in their blood-lust, yet stern in their profession,
Hardened men of iron grit and fiery hot aggression,

Machine guns rattle, mortars thump, and rockets race through the air,
Tis the obdurate orchestra of death, the sanguine symphony of warfare,
Commanders composing their grisly songs as riflemen charge through the din,
Every band of boys too anxious to prove that they be men,

Ravaging the bloody fields and slaying every foe,
The grunt holds to his brothers, the greatest love he knows,
Honor bound to keep his oaths and allegiance to his Corps,
This be the march of infantry, the vocation of death and war.

GRATITUDE

A quiet but powerful god, only found with sedulous searching,
Conjured but by the few, in their devout and determined urging,
Forgotten does it often live to those of pessimistic mind,
For no amount of godsent gifts can they ever seem to find,

Obeisance must be paid in full, at the laudation of the dawn,
Or with every nocturne prayer 'fore the curtains of night are drawn,
Yet It's sacrifice is meager, one need but look away,
From the ashes of the past and the shadows of the day,

It's glory may seem small but it's boon is bright and blooming,
And the more that one invokes it, the greater is it's looming,
Casting back those blackened veils that shroud empty mortal eyes,
Reminding Man of lustrous life and spurring his spirit to rise,

Humble stands that halcyon god, patient at its post,
Munificent to its pious cult as their favored fecund host.

HOUNDS OF WAR

Forged in the crucible of fire and blood,
Fell deeds destroying men in the fields of mud,
Death incarnate they prowl killing grounds,
Barking and bloody like feral hell-hounds,
Here treads the infantry of that violent corps,
Bred for one purpose and that purpose is war.

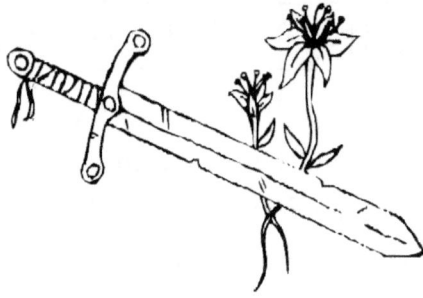

THE DUALITY OF MAN

Not long gone are the days when men poeticized and painted,
Or sculpted and sung, for they and art were well-acquainted,
For they could fight and they could dance, and gain glory on all fronts,
Wresting renown from all manner of stunts,

Fighting men were poets and many writers went to war,
A man cloaked in color could soon be covered in gore,
Great thinkers there were that could wield many an arm,
Knowing how to create and how to fight with great harm,

All the great works in both music and prose,
Were beget by men who could plan and compose,
For every famed building and hallowed book,
Demanded a man with a higher outlook,

Masculine was the daring deed of creation,
And many a man embraced such a station.

IKON OF THE FATHER

An ikon of the sublime world, like a portal to heaven's vault,
Supreme arbiter of familial affairs, leading his cherished cult,
Giving glimpse of godly grace, lord incarnate in his own home,
Peer to others in shared land, but sovereign under domestic dome,

Enraptured does his consort sit, beside him in his stately throne,
Her wisdom matching beauty yet the decision is his alone,
For counsel she does offer him with guidance soft and feminine,
Dutiful in her eminent place, for here he stands 'bove other men,

Descendants of his blooded line, run flush about his fruitful fief,
For he walks amongst them as a god, instilling them with blest belief,
Watching wistfully from below, longing to become what they see,
Protector, provider, and leader, and all else that they could be,

A man with such an onus, may find meaning in such a weight,
And though he be mere mortal, fatherhood may elevate his state.

SELF-YOKED

Man is a bull, a beast of earth and field,
Bold and unbroken he treads under the sun,
Reverent and beaming in its golden yield,
Loyal to his own and yoked by none,

With strength and courage he proudly stands,
Amongst the bulls of his own he finds his place,
Bound together they enliven their land,
Leading with wisdom and virile grace,

The load that he bears is heavy in weight,
Yet it's borne of his own volition and will,
To become a man to which others gravitate,
And to intractably live to his own ravenous fill,

Man is a bull when his virtue's invoked,
Unbent and red-blooded, standing self-yoked.

SKYWARD VISION

Upwards facing, towards the excellent,
Towards that which is better and brighter,
Never possessed by ressentiment,
Focused on striving ever higher.

RISING TIDE

A sincere compliment, a friendly nod,
A gesture of faith, a praise to God,
A welcoming smile and a gracious greeting,
A hearty laugh in a passing meeting,

Cordial care to strangers leaving,
Empathy to close friends grieving,
Patience with your upset kin,
Recognition when your rivals win,

Charity when you're penniless,
Untroubled when you fall or miss,
Uplifting when your heart is low,
Humble when there's more you know,

For a rising tide lifts all ships,
And a brimful cup can spare some drips,
And even if the waters slim,
A bit of heart can raise all men.

BROKEN BUT UNBOWED

In all my travels and distant treks,
I've seen strength and endurance at its apex,
Claimed by the few who wake every day,
Full of pain and suffering that naught can allay,

Their body broken or in total revolt,
So beleaguered they are that every breath is a jolt,
Plagued by accident or chronic disease,
Never offered a moment of rest nor ease,

Yet choosing to rise with every dawn,
Unwilling to yield when their health is gone,
For their spirit is made of mettle and grit,
The human soul on fire refusing to quit.

A LETTER TO WOMEN

Dear women of the world, this letter's written out with care,

For I understand your protests and your thoughts brought about by fear,

Men admire and respect you, asking not for serfs or slaves,

But your way is lost and twisted and many now cannot be saved,

For you are creatures bright and beautiful, having strength and power plenty,

But the forms those virtues take, are not just all and any,

The power that you wield is both indirect and subtle,

But can topple nations in its force and spur men to hellish struggle,

How many men your powers felled or lifted up like gods,

Or brought off from the brink, men fighting desperate odds,

A power not of manly might nor charging acts of gall,

But a power just the same, affecting one and all,

Your strength and grit cause wonder, but not by might of arm or nerve,

For the blade of the sword is forceful, but maybe not as much as the curve,

While your presence alone draws destiny, and your voice charms monsters and men,

Your prowess is measured in grace and not by the scars on your glowing skin,

For the endurance of women is stunning, their patience in hardship and need,

And their talent for keeping their softness, while plagued by fell and dreadful deed,

No one cares if you outwork or out lift a burly brute,
Nor climb the corporate ladder in a dashing three piece suit,
You can try to run the trenches with the bold and virile youth,
Or win scientific laurels in pursuit of fact and truth,
But the qualities you trade to be but mediocre men,
Denies you of your virtues gifted to the feminine,

And yes there's a double standard but that road goes both ways fast,
It's not a competition for either sex to outshine those outside their class,
Men love you for the feminine that you embody at your best,
Not emulating men in some warped and futile contest,
For mountains will be moved and the heavens will be rent,
By men who see a woman in her natural bent,

A bastion for the weary and a rock within the storm,
The hearth within the home, enlivening and warm,
Your solace a kind salve, to which men and children flock,
Your company and joy of the greatest loving stock,
So radiant your laughter, casting back the gloom,
A wife and selfless mother, carrying the future in her womb,

And yes a man I be, and know not of all your pain,
But the pursuit to be like men, will be but strength spent in vain,
If you embrace your feminine worth, rejecting rivalry of sex,
You'll climb a different mount, where you can reach the fair apex,
For the grace and beauty of women has more power than you know,
And what's even more is the great worth and love it can bestow.

INVOCATION OF WILL

Sometimes when the days are bleak,

And your body's heavy and your limbs are weak,

When exhaustion takes you in its grip,

And your mind is low in a murky dip,

You must muster up some cloistered will,

Until heart now pumps it's life bloods fill,

Breaking through that bleary breach,

To attain the life within your reach,

Counting not on ghosts or gods,

Nor even limbs too weary to plod,

But conjuring up that mortal flame,

That rips like lightning through your veins,

A deeper strength that seems to beat,

With defiant ardor and burning heat,

Not for glory nor laurels won,

But simply to do what must be done.

THE GOLDEN FALL OF ICARUS

Gallant, golden Icarus how in your daring you did fly,
Rising above your station, not afraid to touch the sky,
Striving ever boldly, yet vainly was it so,
To become more than you were in your fated feat of woe,

Yet who can blame a restive youth, with ambition great and grand,
Striving towards a vision that few can see or understand,
So imbued with purpose, that charge upon the heights,
Who's to say his venture wasn't worth his foredoomed plight,

For he soared above the clouds in his bold and burning need,
So desperate to enthrone his name by audacious act and deed,
That even in his downfall there was still virtue to behold,
As the Sun he had dared to rival still cast his body In gleaming gold.

LAW OF THE THUNDERBOLT

In the course of nature the thunder bolt guides all,
So as the brunt of thrusted spear or the cudgel as it falls,
Exacts the violent verdict by the right of tooth and claw,
It thereby makes itself both first and final law.

CHANGING COURSE

The river winds and races, relentless through the land,
In its restless route to strike the stark and salty strand,
Single-minded in its purpose and its need to reach the sea,
To only that one end could the river ever be set free,

Yet the land is hard and rigid, demanding water change its course,
Equal to the river with its own unyielding force,
Driving that deluge to but rip another trail,
So that sometimes to another sea the river must prevail,

In this lies all the danger that the river could ever face,
For the lakes and ponds will tempt it to settle in their place,
Now that it's course is longer, and weaving far afield,
Its flow could slack and stagnate, enticing it to yield,

And so in its flux of passage, it's purpose it may lose,

For that one sea was its aim, so boundless and so blue,

Yet if it keeps it's fluent flex, and it's unflinching forward motion,

It will find that every sea is synonymous with the ocean.

GRAY OF FEATHER

There are two types of birds in every place and clime,
Both grey in weathered feather, long past their fledgling prime,
Some hobble on the ground, some still soar the lofty heights,
Some wallow in their nests, some still revel in their flights,

Many a hoary bird simply laze upon their perch,
Or pick upon the ground, in a dull and listless search,
Incessantly they squawk, but never share a crooning song,
Relinquishing their grace and the bounty of the strong,

Yet other birds, though few, may still fill the lucid skies,
Or strut in august pride with lusty gleaming eyes,
Serenading in their hymns, of wisdom and of vim,
Relishing in their waning yet still potent strength of limb,

For the weather-beaten bird has two paths from which to choose,
To be subdued by the storm, or remain steadfast and refuse,
To lose its full and vibrant feathers either bitter or insipid,
Or fly as inspiration on lusty currents, hearty and committed.

IDEALS ABOVE

Live to fight another day,
That's what the wisemen say,

Forget the oaths that you swore,
There be no deeds worth dying for,

Sacrifice is all in vain,
And heroism grants no gain,

Folly is the pious death,
Nothing's higher than human breath,

Never make a final stand,
In loyalty to faith or land,

No belief should usurp life,
Conviction only leads to strife,

Yet ugly are the wiseman's ways,
Against high ideals they inveigh,

Now death is not the apex aim,
But some beliefs are worth the claim,

For what is life if nothing's higher,
Just a pointless game till you expire,

Is nothing sacred that you hold,
No modern faith nor gods of old,

Don't you bear some manly creed,
To spur you on toward dauntless deed,

Or live a code you will not break,
No matter of the fate at stake,

Be there not a single hill,
That you'd defend with Iron-will,

Must you have such certainty,
To believe in something earnestly,

Is life the grandest of your gods,
With nothing greater that you laud,

Or could there be a greater love,
For some belief way up above,

A burning passion of the soul,
Beyond the price of corporal toll,

For over life there are those few,
Ideals above our mortal view.

PASSION NEEDS NO CONVINCING

"I don't want to," is that not enough,

Why offer to yourself some convoluted bluff,

Or dissect that simple phrase as if there's more to learn,

As if the subject of those words is for what you truly yearn,

For you shouldn't need convincing of what you really want,

No matter of the potency with which that aim does haunt,

Not every deed needs dared, nor every mountain climbed,

Your span of life is fleeting one second at a time,

So why not face those fears that bar you from your way,

Taking to those trails on which your passion can not stray,

There be goals that you aspire to and ends that you do seek,

And if there's fear or laziness, you must confront what's weak,

Surmounting all those faults on your quest to reach your aim,

But if it's not the goal you want then quitting brings no shame,

For you may have set a goal so lofty in your head,

But from a change of heart placed another in its stead,

And now feel a gnawing pressure biting at your core,

As if in your constant changing you forsook what you stood for,

But the crux of life is change and so too your wants and hopes,

And to say that you don't want to is not some simple cope.

RAYS OF SERENITY

A soft afternoon,
Sunlight drifting through the trees,
Time is in a lull.

HELIOCENTRIC

The Sun worries not of bigger stars,
They pose no threat so distantly far,
Only looking to them for proud emulation,
Never to shame its own noble station,

For it makes of itself a blinding light,
A magnetic force in its own proud right,
The core of its cosmos with single aim,
To burn in the darkness with fervent flame,

It flares and it flashes with fulgent fire,
Stoking it's blaze ever higher,
Reverent to those of richer ray,
But assured of itself as the bringer of day.

GOLDEN PHASES

Behold the burning sun, bursting bright above,
Bathing the world in glory as a golden glyph thereof,
An alluvion of light, enlivening to all,
In its high halcyon phase, bearing blessèd windfall,

Yet periods of sublime skies, when life is large and grand,
Must inevitably recede, when night falls upon the land,
Giving way to darkness and ever deeper gloom,
Till the only light remaining is the pallor of the moon,

But like a beacon midst the black, reflecting flame of day,
It keeps loyal to the luster of lofty solar rays,
So that even in the shadowed pitch there be a glint of sun,
Holding the dread position, until dawn again has come,

Breaking through the blackened breach, flares the rage of morn,
Ushering in a vital age, its golden phase reborn,
The cycle of the cosmic, ceaseless in its shifting,
With times of dreadful darkness and days with light uplifting.

DIFFERENT PATH, DIFFERENT MOUNTAIN

Every path is different, in this the truths been told,
But so is every mountain, no matter of the goal,
For the tragedy of man is to climb his fated peak,
But once upon the summit feel inadequate and meek,
For he's glimpsed the lofty mountains with higher climbs and treks,
And thus looks upon his own as some insignificant speck,

He neither curses nor degrades the ascendant acts of men,
Never mocks nor ridicules the summits that they win,
But feels a quiet gnawing despite his alpine trail,
Unable to reconcile the differences in scale,
Forgetting that his path and thus his destined mount,
Is developed by a life sprung from a different fount,

Indeed his eyes should wander to see those of men above,
Yet only for inspiration and the emulation thereof,

To look for higher mountains and elevate his plans,

But not corrupt his worth or his standing as a man,

For its true that there be betters across this mortal plane,

But the complexity of life means no two mounts can be the same.

A TITAN AMONGST PYGMIES

Deep in the wild woods there rose a tiny city,
The paltry, squalid home of the modern, western Pygmy,
Where friends and neighbors fought, keeping others down,
Lest some daring doer attain laurels of renown,

But striding through the brush one day appeared a towering Titan,
Bearing gifts of plenty to both inspire and enlighten,
Moving mountains with his hands and redirecting rivers,
So that the city could ascend with the bounty he delivered,

Yet in his gracious greatness the shadow cast was long,
And the pygmies could not stand him so prominent and strong,
So despite their acrid village, in this they could agree,
The Titan must come down and bend his haughty knee,

With ropes and chains they caught him in the overwhelming swarm,
Demanding he submit, languish and conform,
Now shackled to the ground and entangled in their snare,
The Titan suffered ridicule and every vile swear,

Picking out his flaws like vultures gulping vitals,
They profaned his mighty works and maligned his lofty titles,
Till a single Pygmy spoke against the madness of the horde,
For this genius giant he felt was truly worthy of reward,

A Titan I am not he said but need I feel the lesser,

After all his vital virtue need I act as the aggressor,
For his merit is beyond reproach and I am still a man,
Worthy in my own right, without need to fell the grand,

But the pygmies only frenzied, shocked at such a speech,
And the speaker was subdued midst the vitriolic screech,
Thus a prideful Pygmy was lashed upon the ground,
Next to the awesome Titan and his harshly slandered crown,

Thus many a life was lost that day, the Titan and the Pygmy,
But so too was the spirit forever from the city,
For they slayed the epic Titan and bashed his splendid name,
All on the account that they could not bear the shame,

Lest it be forgotten those daring dynamos,
Cast their glowing glory to exalt those far below,
So behold the noble Titan, that rare specimen of man,
That avatar of virtue, the sun shining where he stands,
His works worthy of renown, his ideal a light to all,
A source of inspiration if not toppled in the fall.

FORCE AND FLUIDITY

Flame of fateful fire, ripping 'cross the tract,
Relentless in your rush and single-minded act,
Bursting through the barriers that dare to bar your way,
Like a blazing juggernaut blasting through the fray,

Wave of lissome water, flowing through the land,
Confident that your course will reach the salty strand,
Persistent in your purpose yet fluid in your form,
Like an oceanic Titan moving with the wild storm,

Those elemental forces duly driving in your quest,
Each a potent power in their particular contests,
Suited for different stages towards ends that you aspire,
With times for rolling water and those for raging fire.

SEMPRONIUS DENSUS: SOL'S CENTURION

Lo! Sol Invictus do tell me the tale,
Of that steadfast centurion whose faith never failed,
For only he was the one that you hailed that dark day,
Whose solemn honor and oath he refused to betray,

Stalwart Sempronius, the praetorians best,
For this is the truth of the man elysian blessed,
A grizzled soldier of Rome staunchly sworn to his ward,
Who alone attempted to defend his charge from the horde,

For there in the street marched the emperor and heir,
Guarded by the throng of Caesar's legionnaires,
Till a swarm of assassins swarmed the stark scene,
Brandishing their swords with a sinister sheen,

But the bodyguards broke and deserted their post,
Or corrupted their oaths and joined the foul host,
Save for Sempronius who defiantly stood,
Wickedly wielding his staff of vine-wood,

While no imperial friendship did he ever share,
Nor relish raptly in the regime's political glare,
He still stood as Aeneas for his fealty held fast,
Forsaken in the fray but towering and vast,

With a strong, booming voice he rebuked the cruel crowd,

While to his honor and duty he silently vowed,
Till the assailants did press and his dagger was drawn,
His countenance blazing like the fiery dawn,

Now in the midst of the mass Sempronius raged,
His single act worthy of a rich, golden age,
For so bold was his stand and so fierce was his fight,
Sol Invictus looked down and commended his plight,

Yet if truth must be known, and the truth is quite bleak,
Both the emperor and his heir were cut down in the street,
But even worse was Sempronius when brought to the ground,
For he alone held allegiance when treachery was abound,

Though doomed was his deed and black was his bane,
His devotion and valor were not spent in vain,
For man's virtue and value are deathless and bright,
Forever aflame like stars in the night.

KISS OF THE SUN

Warmth of sun on skin,
Is there any greater joy,
All is well in life.

THE MARROW OF LIFE

Here in the flesh I stand, both in the valley and upon the peak,
Come to claim within my single life the greatness that I seek,
Though many a man may rival me I have naught but my own to prove,
For here I stand a self-yoked man with not but my soul to lose,
And shall I sink into the pit to never crawl out again,
Let that blackness take me in its grip for that be the ultimate sin,

But if in that darkness I do rise, to climb the earthen wall,
And yet still knowing once again I will meet that dire fall,
Then the light that comes to greet me as I crawl upon the sward,
Will lavish me in more golden hues than I can blissfully afford,
Reminding me of righteous aims that I do strive to claim,
Setting once again both my heart and soul aflame,

For when that sun does ravage me with calloused grace and care,
Only generous to those who boldly bear their mortal share,
Then trudging up the heights again until swiftly I do race,
I find upon the mountaintop my-self and proper place,
Granted all the goodness of this bright and corporal realm,
Straining to stay upon my feet, I'm so nearly overwhelmed,

Below me spans the vastness of opportunity and chance,
As I feel the waxing and the wonder from my own burgeoning expanse,
Power pumping through my veins like lightning of the storm,
An envoy of the sky-god in thunderous human form,
Charged with mighty deeds that challenge and incite,

Driving me towards excellence in my own exalted plight,

Inheritor of sublime life in all its fleeting splendor,
Carrying the immortal fire that my fathers once did render,
Taking embers of the past to blaze a bright new trail,
With the glory of the fire that must undoubtedly prevail,
Casting back all blackness and assailing every foe,
To win this life of plenty as great men did long ago,

I may not be the paragon of righteousness and worth,
But still an avatar I am, heaven sent upon this earth,
Striving ever upward in-spite of mortal coil,
Relishing in bold enterprise filled with risk and toil,
Come to claim what's rightfully mine by virtue of my will,
To suck the marrow from the bone and sate my vital fill,

Greedily I pluck the fruit from every branch of life,
Roaming ever vibrantly in orchards rich and rife,
My feet upon the earthen field, my eyes upon the sky,
Nothing far beyond my reach if only I will try,
Shifting in the lowly valleys up to the lofty mounts,
Forever do I gladly thirst, drinking from the fount.

www.ingramcontent.com/pod-product-compliance
Lightning Source LLC
LaVergne TN
LVHW052018080426
835513LV00018B/2075